HearinG

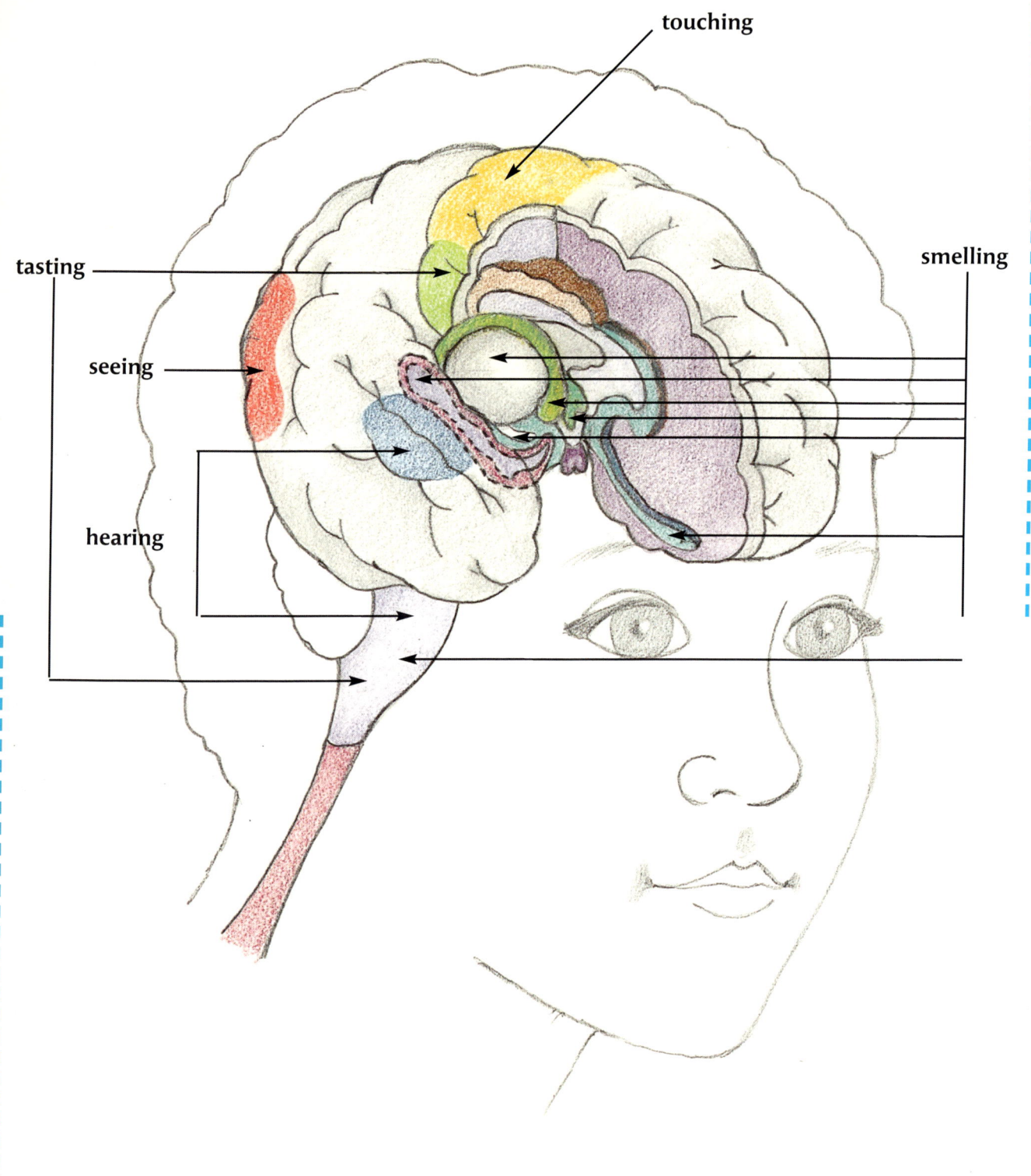

Hearing

Dr. Alvin Silverstein, Virginia Silverstein,
and Laura Silverstein Nunn

Senses and Sensors
Twenty-First Century Books
Brookfield, Connecticut

Cover and interior illustrations by Anne Canevari Green
Photographs courtesy of © The Image Works: p. 8 (Bob Daemmrich); © Visuals Unlimited: pp. 10 (D. Yeske), 34 (SIU), 48 (Max Honn); © Merlin D. Tuttle, Bat Conservation International: p. 11; © Peter Arnold, Inc.: pp. 13 (Leonard Lessin), 20 (BIOS); © Phototake: pp. 17 (John Dudak), 45 (Richard Nowitz); © Photo Researchers, Inc.: pp. 18 (William H. Mullins), 29 (Richard Hutchings), 38 (Action for Disability, Newcastle upon Tyne/Simon Fraser/SPL), 41 (Russell D. Curtis), 42 (Bachmann), 52 (Kairos, Latin Stock/SPL), 54 (James King-Holmes/SPL)

Library of Congress Cataloging-in-Publication Data
Silverstein, Alvin.
Hearing / by Alvin Silverstein, Virginia Silverstein, and Laura Nunn.
p. cm. — (Senses and sensors)
Includes bibliographical references and index.
ISBN 0-7613-1666-3 (lib. bdg)
1. Hearing—Juvenile literature. [1. Hearing. 2. Ear. 3. Senses and sensation.] I. Silverstein, Virginia B. II. Nunn, Laura Silverstein. III. Title. IV. Series.
QP462.2 .S578 2001   573.8'9—dc21   2001018107

Published by Twenty-First Century Books
A Division of The Millbrook Press, Inc.
2 Old New Milford Road
Brookfield, Connecticut 06804
www.millbrookpress.com

Text copyright © 2001 by Dr. Alvin Silverstein,
Virginia Silverstein, and Laura Silverstein Nunn
Illustrations copyright © 2001 by Anne Canevari Green
All rights reserved
Printed in the United States of America
5 4 3 2 1

Contents

Chapter One
SOUNDS ALL AROUND 9

Chapter Two
HEARING SOUNDS 12

Chapter Three
IT'S ALL IN THE BRAIN 24

Chapter Four
SPEAKING AND LISTENING 31

Chapter Five
THE SOUND OF MUSIC 40

Chapter Six
SEEING WITH SOUND 46

Chapter Seven
TOO MUCH SOUND? 50

GLOSSARY 56

FURTHER READING 60

INTERNET RESOURCES 61

INDEX 62

HearinG

The sense of hearing is very important in helping us learn about the world around us. How do you feel when you hear a band play music? Is it soothing, disruptive, exciting, or enlightening? Our brains interpret what we hear as the sounds relate to our daily lives.

ONE
Sounds All Around

You wake up to the sound of an alarm clock blaring in your ears. You hear the leaves rustle outside your window on a windy morning. You recognize the sound of your friend's voice as she yells your name from across the school hallway. At the sound of the school bell, you know that the class is over and it's time to go home. On the way home, you have a conversation with a friend on a school bus packed with noisy students. At bedtime, you keep hearing the leaky faucet go "drip, drip," and it seems so loud that you have trouble falling asleep. In the middle of the night, your cat knocks a heavy book off the desk in your bedroom and you wake up startled.

Throughout the day and even into the night, sounds surround us. Our ears tune in to thousands of different kinds of sounds. Some provide information that we may need for survival—the sudden blast of a smoke alarm, for example; others are just "background noise" that we hear but don't pay attention to.

Everything we know about the world comes through our five main senses—seeing, hearing, smelling, tasting, and touching. In this book, we will discuss the sense of hearing and its importance in helping us to learn about the world around us. Whether we are listening to the sound of a blue jay chirping in the backyard, a telephone ringing, or the loud beat of drums in the school band, our mind receives impressions of the world. The messages from our ears and other sense organs are interpreted by the brain and turned into meaningful information.

DID YOU KNOW?

Next to vision, humans depend most on the sense of hearing.

Sounds provide important information that we rely on throughout the day. What message does the noise from this object send to your brain?

All living organisms—humans, animals, and even plants—have senses. They gather information about the world through specialized structures called **sensors**. These sensors detect various types of energy and send information about them to the brain to be translated into significant messages: laughter, a ringing phone, a door slamming shut.

As effective as human senses are, however, they are far from the best that nature has evolved. Some animals have senses that far exceed our own. What would it be like, for example, if you could walk through a pitch-dark room without bumping into anything? Or what if you could hear sounds from a considerable distance away? Some animals can do things like that. Owls depend on their remarkable hearing to hunt prey at night. An owl's hearing is so keen that it can pinpoint the sounds of a scurrying mouse in the dark of night as far as a half mile away. Bats use their amazing hearing to "see" at night. They send out sounds that bounce off objects and come back to their ears. These echoes help them to avoid obstacles and locate insects in the dark.

People have developed devices—artificial sensors—to expand our senses to equal or even surpass those of animals. Using sonar systems, submarines can navigate in deep waters, like dolphins and whales, so they can locate objects and avoid obstacles. Acoustic microscopes use sound to help us see very tiny objects. Their sound waves can pass through solids, milky or cloudy liquids, or dark materials. (Microscopes using light waves cannot see through any of these.) Doctors use sound to detect tumors and to look at unborn babies developing inside their mothers' bodies.

Animals have many ways of using their keen sense of hearing to their advantage. Bats are able to catch food at night by sending out sounds that bounce off objects and return to their ears. In this way bats are able to determine where the object is located.

TWO
Hearing Sounds

If you closed your eyes and listened very carefully, could you hear a bee buzzing by, or a cricket chirping, or a friend whispering in your ear? Of course you would notice the blare of a marching band or the loud sounding of a fire alarm. We can recognize many different sounds. How do we do this?

Specialized sensors inside the ears detect sounds, which stimulate nerve signals that are then sent to the brain for processing. The brain interprets the incoming signals and turns them into something we can understand.

What Is Sound?

The sounds we hear are a form of energy. Scientists define energy as the capacity to do work; for example, to move an object. In the case of sound energy, air molecules are being moved.

When a string on a guitar is plucked, the string moves back and forth. This movement is called a **vibration**. When the string vibrates, it presses on gas molecules in the surrounding air. Normally these molecules are spread out, but the vibration pushes them close together (compresses them). These molecules bump into each other and then hit neighboring molecules. The vibration is carried outward from the string, creating waves in the air molecules. When some of the vibrating air molecules hit your eardrum, you can then hear a sound. All sounds make vibrations. If you touch your throat while you are talking, you can feel the vibrations in your voice box. Without vibrations, there is no sound.

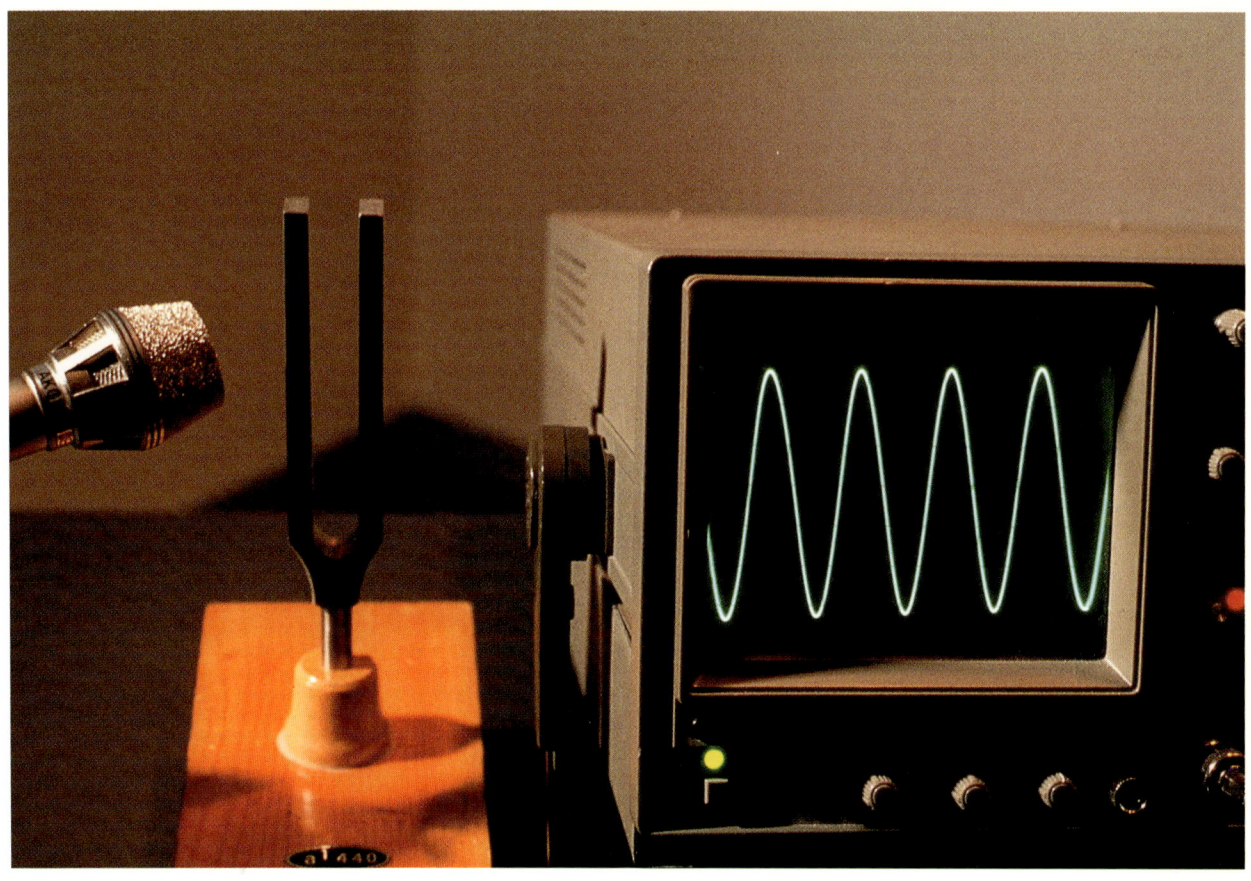

Sound energy can only travel through substances, such as gas, liquid, or solid, because the sound waves (shown here) are sent out by the vibrations of the substance it travels through.

Sound energy is similar to light energy in that they both travel in waves. Sound waves are called **compression waves** because the molecules in the air are compressed (pushed closer together) when they vibrate. The vibrating object sends out sound waves in all directions. Sound energy, however, cannot travel through a vacuum (such as the emptiness of outer space) the way light energy can. Instead, sounds must travel through a medium (a substance), which may be a gas (such as air), a liquid, or a solid. Sound travels faster through liquids and solids than through gases. The molecules in a gas are farther apart, so it takes more time for them to bump into other molecules than it does in a liquid or solid. In fact, sound travels about four times faster through water and about fifteen

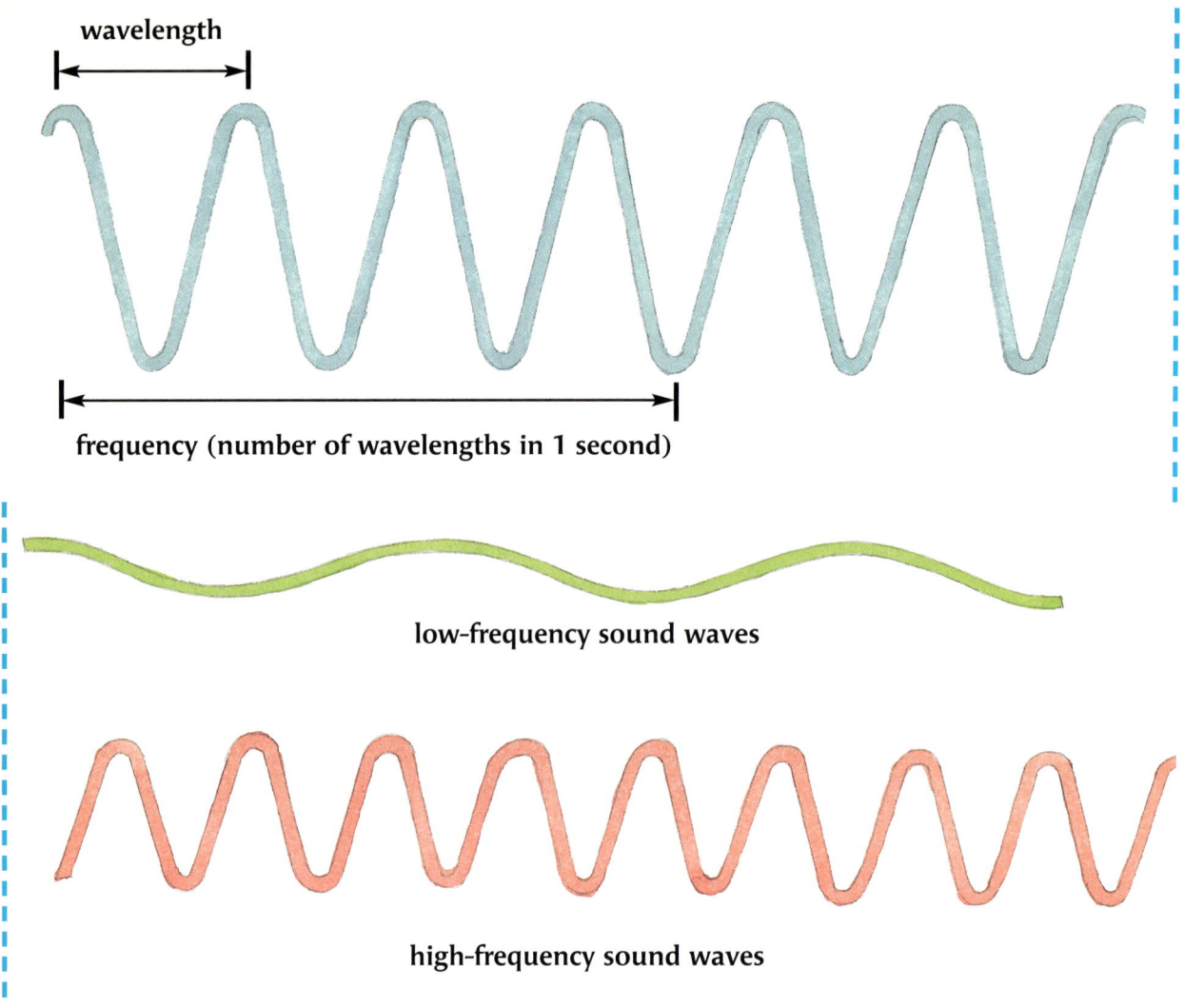

times faster through steel. Have you ever seen a Western movie in which a Native American puts his ear to the ground to hear the distant hoofbeats of horses? He put to use the fact that sound travels faster through solid ground than it does through air.

The nature of sounds is determined by their wavelengths. A **wavelength** is the distance between one compression (wave peak) and the next one. The number of waves produced by a vibrating object each second is called the **frequency** of the sound waves. The faster an object vibrates, the greater the frequency. As the frequency increases, the wavelength decreases. Scientists use the unit **hertz** (or cycles per second) to measure frequency. Most people can hear sounds from about 20 hertz—very low tones—up to 20,000 hertz—very high tones. A person's voice can produce frequencies from 85 to 1,100 hertz. Animals such as bats, dogs, and dolphins can hear **ultrasounds**—sounds with frequencies far above 20,000 hertz. And some animals, such as elephants, can make sounds with frequencies too low for humans to hear. These are called **infrasounds**. Elephants use infrasounds to communicate with other elephants several miles away. Whales also communicate with infrasounds. Their "songs" travel rapidly through the ocean water and can be heard by other whales hundreds of miles away!

The frequency of a sound determines its **pitch**—how high or low a sound seems to a listener. High-pitched sounds have higher frequencies than lower-pitched sounds. When you turn an electric fan on "low," its blades move rather slowly, and you hear a low-pitched hum. If you turn the fan up to a higher setting, the blades turn more rapidly, causing the air molecules around them to vibrate faster. This produces a higher-frequency sound wave, and you hear a higher-pitched hum. (What do the high-pitched whine of a mosquito and the lower-pitched buzz of a bee tell you about how fast their wings flap?)

When sound waves vibrate, each molecule moves back and forth from its original position. The farther it moves, the greater the amount of energy flowing through the sound waves and the louder the sound seems.

Sound Detectors

Most animals have some sort of structures that can detect sounds. These sound-detecting structures vary a great deal in the animal kingdom, from tiny insects to land and water animals, to humans.

> ### Silence in Space
> In episodes of the *Star Trek* TV series, when the *U.S.S. Enterprise* battled with an alien ship, viewers could hear the sound of blasts coming from the phasers firing between the two ships. But that is not scientifically accurate. Sound can travel only if there are molecules around. There are no molecules in space. Therefore, it is impossible for phasers to make a sound in space. Similarly, real-life astronauts cannot talk to each other directly when they are on the moon. Instead, they must communicate by radio. (Radio waves, like light waves, can travel through a vacuum.)

Did You Know?

Moths can't hear very well when their wings are down, covering their "ears." During flight, they pick up sounds better when their wings are flapping up.

For instance, can you imagine having a pair of ears on your chest? Moths do. Actually, moths don't have true ears but rather two thin membranes that vibrate when sound waves hit them. These work in much the same way as our **eardrums**, the vibrating membranes that stretch across the openings into our ears. A moth's "ears" are located on the front of the body, just below the second pair of wings. The moth has two hearing sensory cells, which work together to pick up ultrasounds—especially bat calls. Bats are the moth's main predators, so sound detection is essential for these insects' survival.

Crickets, like moths, hear with membranes, but their "eardrums" are on their front legs. A cricket points its legs toward a sound it wants to hear. Crickets make sounds by rubbing their legs together, to find a mate or stake out a territory.

Other insects, such as mosquitoes, have sound-detecting structures on their antennae. Tiny hairlike structures, called **hair sensilla**, vibrate in response to low-frequency sounds. Like crickets, mosquitoes use their sense of hearing to find a mate. The vibrations of a female mosquito's wings, beating up and down as she flies, are the sound signal that helps a male find her. But male mosquitoes will also fly toward anything that makes a sound with the same pitch, such as a vibrating tuning fork or the hum of an electric generator.

Ears more like ours are found among the **vertebrates**, which are animals with a backbone and an internal skeleton. (Insects are **invertebrates**; the "skeleton" that supports their body structures is the outer covering of the body.) Some fish hear with a pair of membranes, located on either side of the body. These membranes pick up sound vibrations, which are then carried into a gas-filled sac called the **air bladder**. The vibrations jiggle a series of tiny movable bones that connect the air bladder to the inner ear. Signals are then sent to the fish's brain. We normally think of fish as silent, but when researchers made recordings underwater they discovered that fish make lots of sounds. We do not hear them because the sounds are reflected back into the water when they hit the surface.

Frogs, toads, and other amphibians have ears in a more familiar place—on the sides of their head. Two round disks, just behind a frog's eyes, are sound-sensitive membranes. These are the frog's eardrums. As sounds strike the frog's eardrums, the vibra-

A frog's eardrums are round disks that can be found right behind the frog's eyes.

tions are passed along a small bone that connects to the inner ear, where they are picked up by specialized sensors. Nerve impulses are then sent to the frog's brain to interpret the information. Frogs are well known for the sounds they make. Sounds are produced when air vibrates in their vocal sac (just below the throat). When the frog takes in air, the vocal sac inflates like a bubble and makes the sounds louder so they can be heard at great distances. Frog sounds include mating calls, warning calls, announcements of territory ownership, and responses to other calls.

Most reptiles also have eardrums, from which sound vibrations pass along a small bone into the inner ear. There they are picked up

Bird Songs

Birds inherit their ability to make and interpret songs. Even a songbird raised in isolation will sing; but its song will be rather simple. Normally, birds improve their singing by imitating the songs of other birds of the same species. As they learn the sounds of songs, their own songs become more varied and complex.

by sensors that turn them into nerve messages to be analyzed by the brain. Snakes, however, do not have eardrums and cannot actually "hear" sounds. But they can tell when something is coming near because they feel vibrations in the ground with their jawbones. From vibrations transmitted through the ground, a snake can detect the footsteps of a person yards away. Experiments have shown that snakes also detect low-frequency sounds in the air through vibrations.

Birds have very keen hearing. Their ears are membrane-covered openings on each side of the head, hidden underneath the feathers. Sound vibrations travel along a small rod that is part bone and part cartilage, leading from the eardrum to the inner ear. Hearing is an important part of a bird's life. Birds communicate by singing

A male yellow-headed blackbird lets out a call to declare that this is his territory. Female birds use the males' songs as a kind of fitness test—a male that can sing a variety of complicated songs will probably be a strong and healthy father for her young.

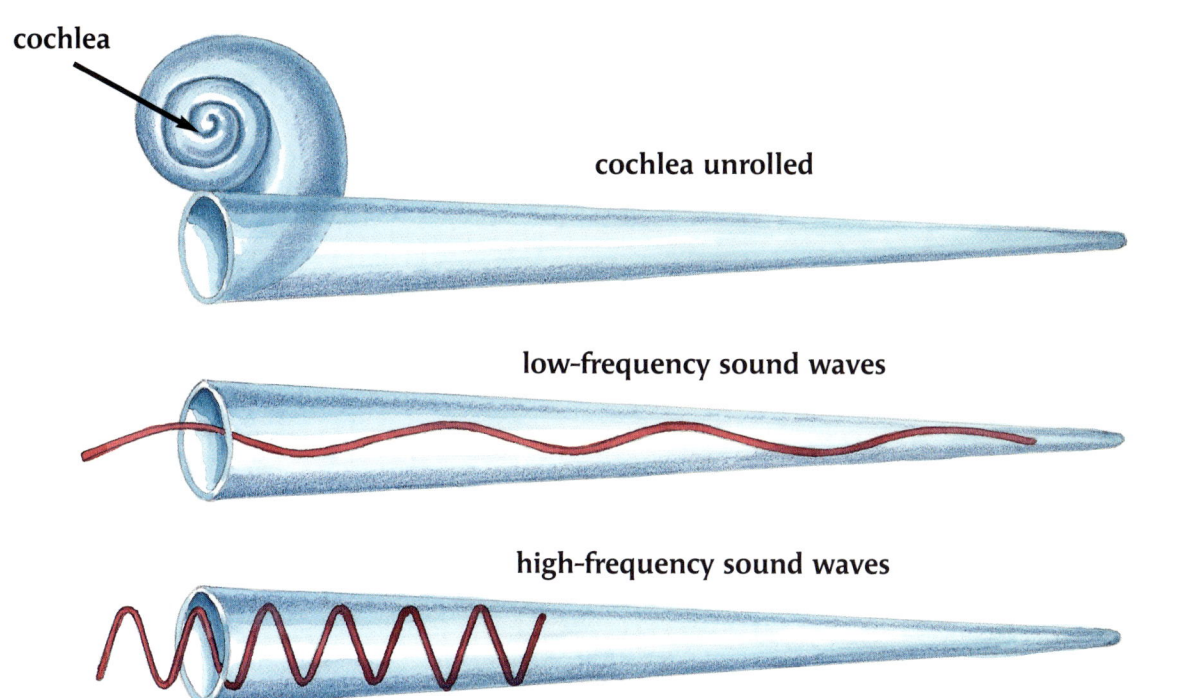

Deep sounds have shallow sound waves that can travel far into the cochlea. Shrill sounds have high frequency sound waves that can only travel a short distance into the narrowing tube. The brain interprets whether the sound is high or low by detecting how far into the cochlea the waves travel.

and also respond to the songs of other birds. These songs are used to establish territory, for courtship, as danger warnings, for finding food, and to communicate with the young.

Mammals' ears (including our own) usually consist of two parts: external ears, called **pinnae**, which extend out from the head; and internal ears, which contain structures to pick up sound vibrations and convert them to nerve messages that are sent on to the brain. These include the eardrum, a sound-sensitive membrane; a series of bones to transmit vibrations inward from the eardrum; and a structure called the **cochlea**, which is lined with delicate hairlike cells that act as sound sensors. Vibrations set the hair cells jiggling against fibers from the **auditory nerve**, which transmits sound messages to the brain.

Did You Know?

Certain animals that live in water, such as sea lions, crocodiles, and hippos, have small ears that they can close when they go below the water surface. This protects the eardrum from the water pressure.

Some animals, such as rabbits, have large curved ears that can send sounds directly into the ear. You can hear better, too, if you cup your hand behind your ear, funneling the sounds into it.

Mammals' outer ears come in all shapes and sizes, but they all do the same job: gathering sound vibrations. Many animals have special muscles that can move their outer ears to collect sound more effectively. Have you ever noticed a dog or horse pricking up its ears when it is alert? It can raise its ears, lower them, and turn them like a satellite-dish antenna, pointing them at an interesting sound.

Humans have ear-moving muscles, too, but most of us can't use them. Even if you can wiggle your ears, you can't turn them toward sounds the way a dog or horse can. Animals such as bats, foxes, and rabbits have large curved ears that channel sounds directly into the ear, just as a funnel helps to channel liquids into the narrow neck of a bottle.

How We Hear

Just like the ears of other mammals, the human ear acts as a sound-gathering device. The outer ear has a large earflap and narrow opening, which help to channel sounds into the inner parts of the ear. After traveling through a tube called the **ear canal**, the sound waves hit the **tympanic membrane,** or eardrum.

The eardrum is extremely sensitive and will vibrate with even the slightest pressure. As the eardrum vibrates, it sends sound waves into the middle ear. The middle ear contains three tiny bones

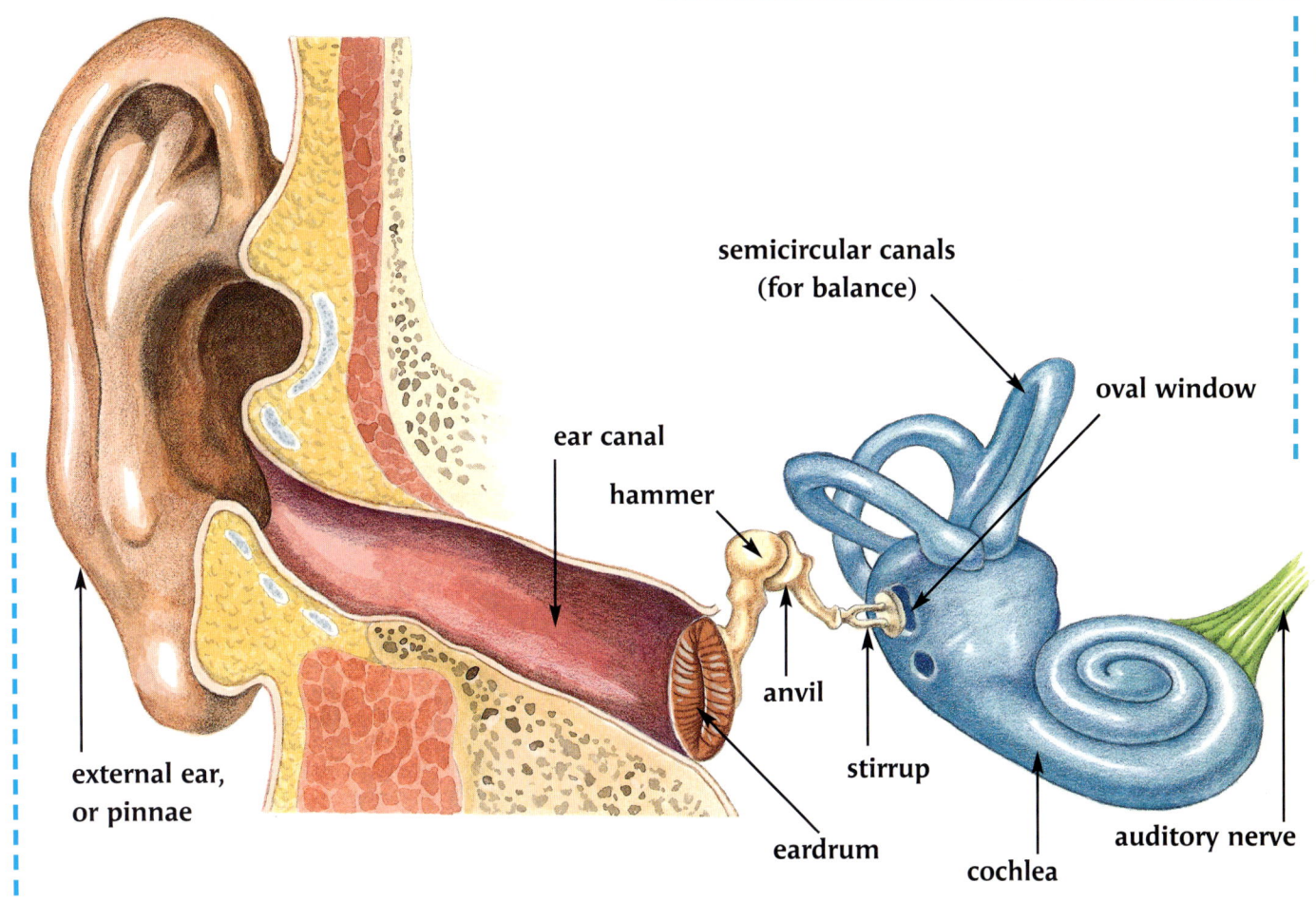

loosely attached together in a row, called the hammer, the anvil, and the stirrup, named after the objects they look like. These are the smallest bones in the human body. When the eardrum vibrates, the hammer, which rests on the eardrum, starts to jiggle. The jiggling hammer then strikes the anvil, causing it to vibrate too. The anvil, in turn, transmits the vibrations to the stirrup. The jiggling stirrup then presses against the **oval window**, the membrane that covers the entrance to the inner ear.

The inner ear contains a group of complicated passageways. The part that is concerned with hearing is the cochlea. The cochlea is a fluid-filled tube that looks like a snail shell. When sound vibrations are transmitted through the oval window, a wave of pressure shoots into the fluid in the cochlea. The floor of the cochlea is

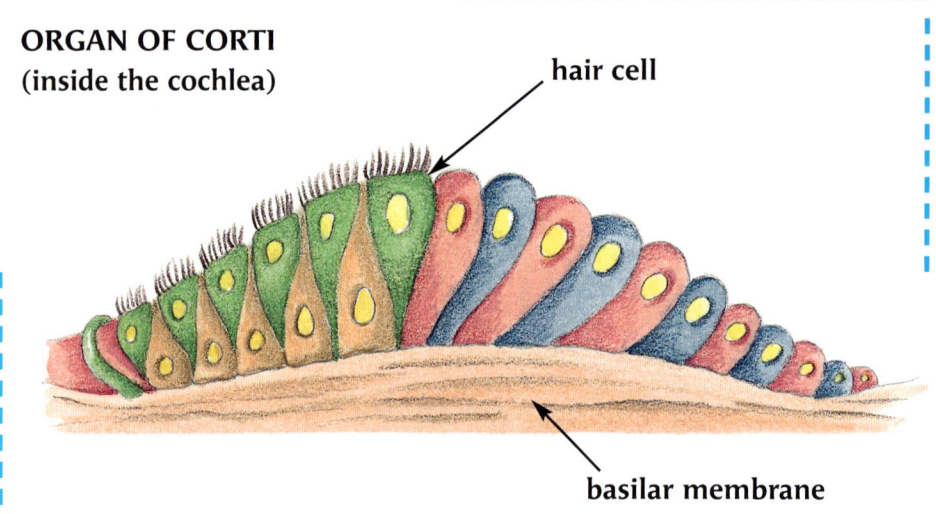

ORGAN OF CORTI
(inside the cochlea)

The organ of Corti rests on top of the basilar membrane. The organ's hair cells bend back and forth as the basilar fibers vibrate.

formed by a membrane called the **basilar membrane**. More than twenty thousand stiff, hairlike fibers are laid out crosswise along this membrane. Like the keys on a xylophone, the basilar fibers are all different sizes, arranged in order from the shortest ones (just 0.04 mm long) to the longest (0.5 mm). The waves in the fluid make some of the basilar fibers vibrate, depending on the frequency: The shortest fibers vibrate at high frequencies, and the longest ones at low frequencies.

Resting on the basilar membrane is a structure called the **organ of Corti**. It contains thousands of hair cells, which act as sound sensors. The vibrations of the basilar fibers cause the hair cells that rest on them to bend back and forth.

So far, you haven't heard anything. But when the sound vibrations are interpreted by the brain, you can hear and understand what you are hearing. A tiny, threadlike nerve fiber runs from each hair cell in the organ of Corti. When a vibration causes a hair cell to bend back and forth, a message is sent along its nerve fiber. The thousands of tiny nerve fibers from the hair cells are gathered into a rope of fibers called the auditory nerve. Messages are carried along the auditory nerve to the brain. Special areas of the brain are devoted to receiving and analyzing messages sent from the ears. The brain will make sense out of the information.

Working with Sound Energy

For centuries, doctors have listened to the sounds from patients' hearts and lungs to help them diagnose illnesses. In 1816, a French physician made the first stethoscope, a simple device that could clearly pick up sounds from the heart, lungs, or other organs of the body. Today's high-tech instruments have expanded the doctor's range. Modern doctors use pictures made from reflected ultrasounds to produce images of structures within the human body. The use of ultrasound allows doctors to diagnose disorders such as brain tumors, gallstones, and liver diseases. They also use ultrasound "sonograms" to check on the development of unborn children.

Scientists and engineers have created devices to record and reproduce sound. A tape recorder records sounds on a cassette tape by changing sound energy to electrical energy. The tape is made of a plastic coated with iron powder. The microphone in the tape recorder changes the sound into electrical signals, which magnetize the iron powder on the tape. When the tape is played, the recorded magnetic signals are changed back into electric signals, which can be turned into sound with the help of speakers.

Radio stations change sound into electrical signals. The electrical energy is converted to radio waves, which are sent out into the air. The antenna on your radio picks up the radio waves, which are then translated back into electrical energy and then into sounds that can be picked up by our ears. Radio waves are actually all around us, but we cannot detect them because we do not have the appropriate sensors.

THREE
It's All in the Brain

Our ears are effective organs for receiving sounds, but alone, they cannot make sense of what we hear. In fact, all the sounds around us would be meaningless noise if it were not for the brain. Auditory receptors in the ear turn the incoming sound vibrations into nerve signals. The auditory nerve carries these messages to the brain, where they are analyzed and interpreted into sounds that we "hear." Special areas in the brain that determine a sound's pitch and loudness work together with special speech centers so that we can understand and distinguish the different sounds we hear.

We aren't born with a brain able to interpret all the messages from the sense receptors. A baby's brain is constantly learning as it is presented with new experiences. When the brain "hears" a sound, it searches for familiar patterns from past experiences. The brain may even fill in gaps according to assumptions based on previous experiences. If you miss a word or two when someone is talking to you, your brain may supply the missing words so automatically that you may not realize you didn't really hear them. If you hear an unfamiliar sound, you may find yourself puzzling over it until you have found out what it is. Then, if it was something interesting or important, you will recognize the sound the next time you hear it.

How the Brain Hears

Everything about us—our memories, thoughts, plans, attitudes, and personality—is all stored in the brain. The largest part of the brain, with which we think, remember, make decisions, and control

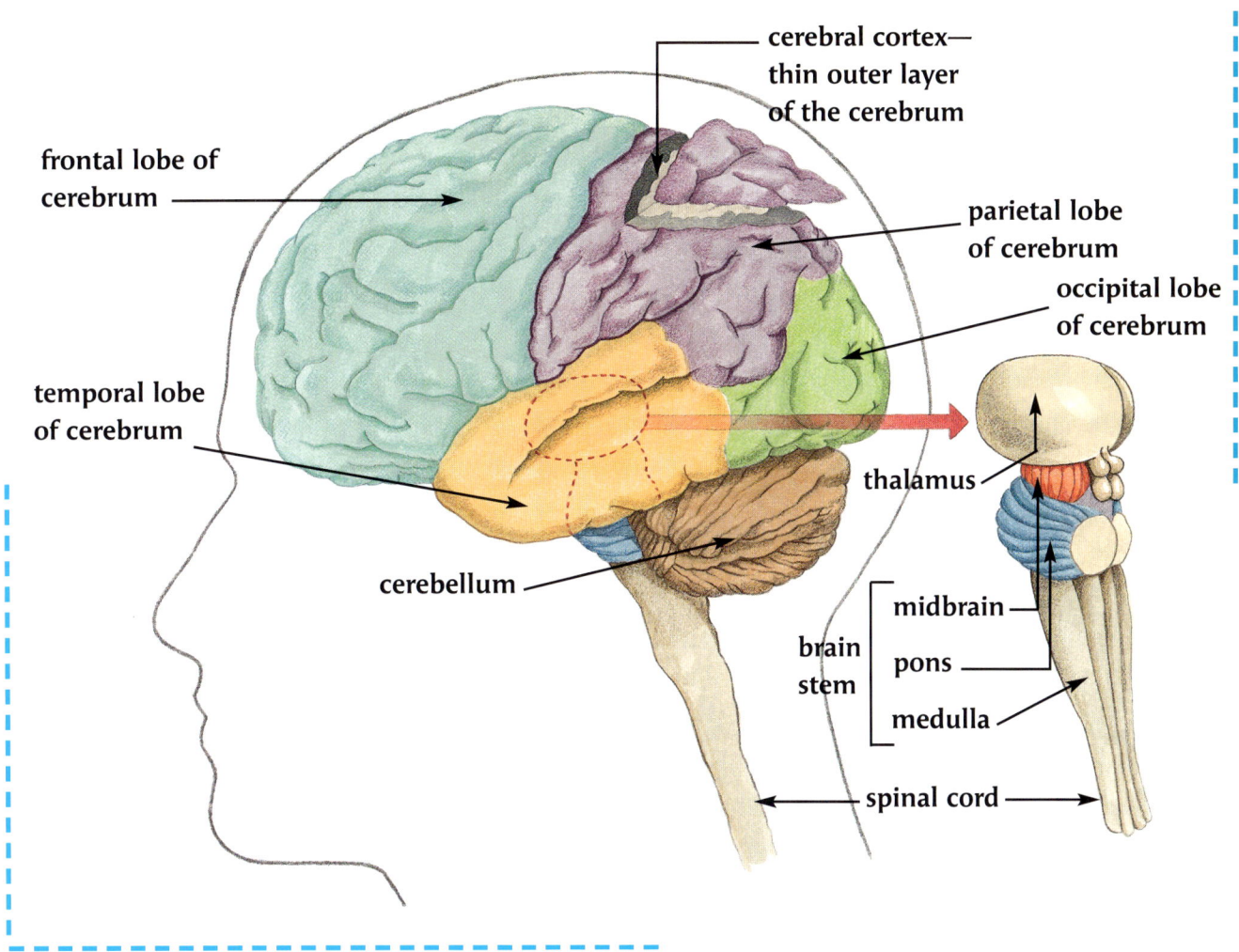

the movements of the body, is called the **cerebrum**. Actually, most of this activity takes place in the **cerebral cortex**, the outermost layer of the brain. This layer, less than 0.25 inch (6 millimeters) thick, contains billions of **neurons** (nerve cells) that receive messages from sense receptors and send out messages to control the activities of the body.

The cerebrum is separated into two halves, the left and right **hemispheres**. The two hemispheres are not completely separate; deep inside the brain, a thick cable of nerve fibers called the **corpus callosum** links the two halves together. Strangely, most of the nerves connecting the cerebrum to the rest of the body cross

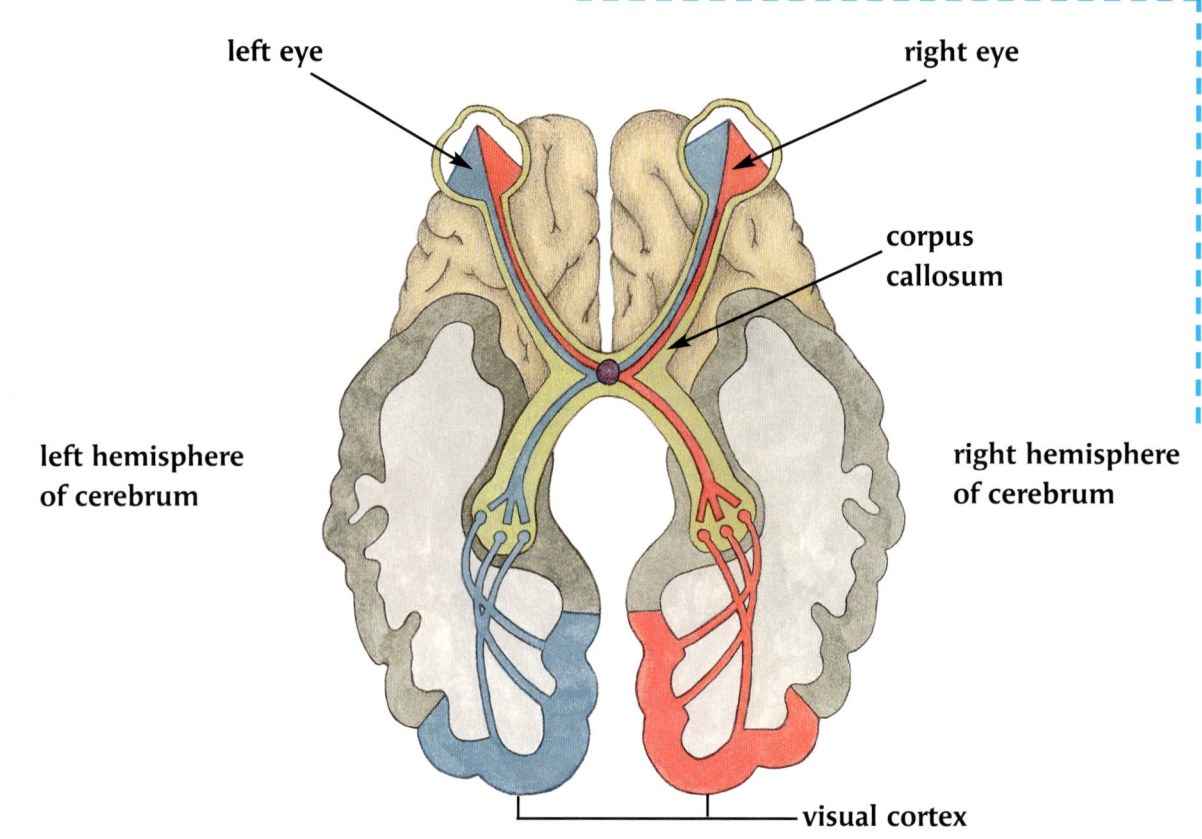

A cutaway view of the interior of the brain shows that the corpus callosum links the left and right hemispheres of the cerebrum.

over to the opposite side as they enter the brain. The brain's crisscross wiring means that movements on the left side of the body are controlled by the right side of the brain, and vice versa, and most of the sense messages that reach each hemisphere come from the opposite side of the body. Some of the messages from the auditory receptors follow this crisscross rule, but some travel up to the hearing center in the same side as the ear. So messages from the left ear go to the hearing centers on both the left and right sides of the brain, and so do those from the right ear. Each hearing center can then compare the impressions from the two ears. Since there are hearing centers on both sides of the brain, and each of them receives sound messages from both ears, even severe damage to one hearing center will not make a person deaf.

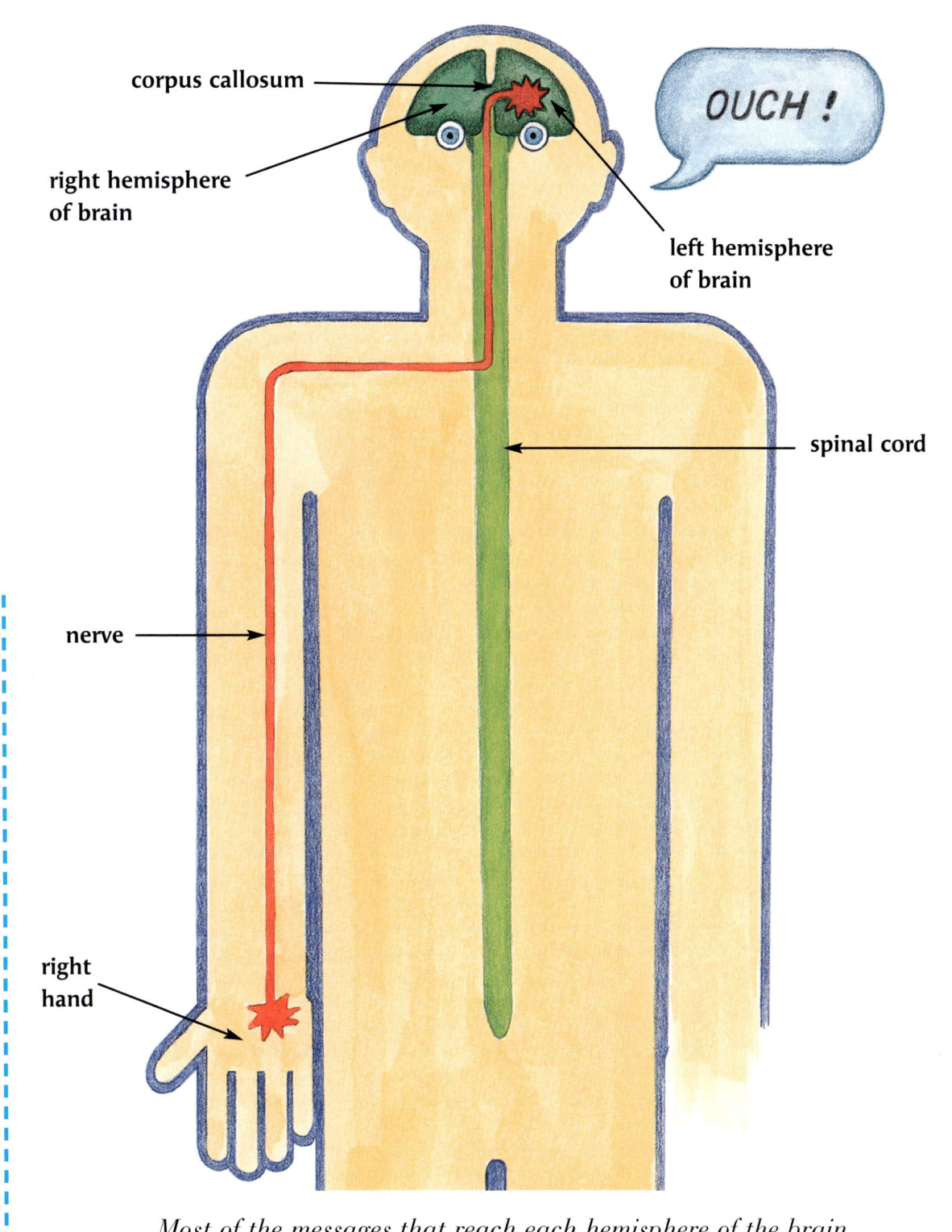

Most of the messages that reach each hemisphere of the brain come from opposite sides of the body.

Did You Know?

What and how you hear may depend on your sex. A recent study using brain scanners showed that when men listen to a story, the hearing center in the left half of the brain is active; but when women listen, their brains typically show activity on both sides. Other studies have found that most women can pay attention to two conversations at once, but most men can't.

Researchers have found that particular areas of the cerebral cortex are associated with specific functions. The part that is involved with hearing is the **auditory cortex**. It is located at the sides of the brain, in the region of each hemisphere called the temporal lobe. If you put both your hands on your head just above your ears, you are touching the parts of your skull that cover the hearing centers. All of the messages from the cochlea are sent to the hearing centers for processing.

Each hearing center has spots that correspond exactly to each point on the basilar membrane in the cochlea. Thus, the brain can determine if a sound was high or low pitched, depending on which hair cells were sending out signals. Nerve messages also carry information on how loud the sounds were. Loud sounds make the nerve cells fire faster. They also excite more hair cells, so that a big noise produces a stronger nerve message. Certain nerve fibers never fire at all unless a sound is especially loud. A message from these hair cells is a signal of a very loud noise. The brain puts all this information together to form a pattern. And at last, you can hear.

Stereo Ears

Cover one of your ears with your hand. What do you hear? Listening through just one ear gives you only part of the sound information. This kind of hearing, called **monaural hearing**, makes it hard to judge the direction and distance of sounds. But in **binaural hearing** (hearing with two ears), each ear hears a sound from a different direction. When you listen to a person's voice, for instance, the two sides of the brain share the information they receive from the two ears. The combined sounds are turned into a single clear, stereo sound.

Binaural hearing is important in finding out which direction a sound is coming from. For example, a sound coming from a source on your right will reach your right ear a fraction of a second before it gets to your left ear. The sound will also be a bit louder in your right ear because it is closer to the sound source. Your brain uses these differences in time and loudness to determine the direction from which the sound is coming. If a sound is directly behind or in front of you, you will need to turn your head to figure out the direc-

The reticular activating system, or RAS, screens all the messages from the senses and sends along only the information that seems important. This way, you can tune out the noises you don't want to hear.

tion of the sound. Animals such as horses, dogs, or bats do not need to do this—they just turn their ears to zero in on the sound.

You can hear the difference between monaural and binaural sound when you listen to tape recordings. A simple tape recording produces a monaural sound, which is flat and not very realistic sounding. Stereo sound uses our ability for sound location to fool the brain. Some sounds produced by a rock band, for example, come from one speaker, and others come from another. When your brain puts together the messages from your right and left ears, it seems more like the "real thing."

29

Did You Know?

A faraway sound seems softer than one coming from a source close to you, so the loudness of a sound gives clues to the distance it has traveled.

Tuning In and Tuning Out

Have your parents ever complained that you didn't do a chore, but you never heard them ask you to do it? Or your mom becomes annoyed when she has to call you three times to get your attention while you are watching TV? Why didn't you hear your parents? Are you going deaf? Of course not. You have no problem hearing them when they ask you if you want to go out for ice cream. And you never miss an invitation to a party. You can hear very well. You just seem to hear what you want to hear.

How is it that you can honestly say you didn't hear your mother ask you to set the table when the sound waves were right there in the air? They traveled down your ear canal, made the eardrum vibrate, were transmitted along the tiny ear bones, went up and down the cochlea, excited all the right hair cells, and sent messages to your brain. Why didn't you hear them?

The answer is in the way the messages from the ears travel through the brain. Before they reach the cerebral cortex, such messages pass through a region in the center of the brain called the **reticular activating system**, or **RAS**. "Reticular" means netlike, and this part of the brain is a net of nerve fibers that acts as a clearinghouse. It screens all the messages from the senses and sends on only those that seem interesting, unusual, or important.

Your RAS permits you to "tune out" the traffic noises on a busy street and have a conversation with a friend, even though your friend's voice may actually be quieter than the roaring cars and trucks. At a party, you can pick out a single voice when many people are talking. The RAS allows you to tune in or tune out any sounds that you want to.

Minor aches and pains often seem to be unbearable at night, and small noises like the ticking of a clock seem more distracting then, because the sense organs are not sending in as much other information. With less competition, the RAS sends these signals through to the higher brain.

When you are asleep, the RAS is turned down, but it is still on duty. Only the most important or startling messages are passed on to the cerebral cortex. You can sleep peacefully through the rumble of trucks, the wail of sirens, the chorus of crickets, and other night sounds, yet you wake instantly if a door slams or a thunderstorm booms outside.

FOUR
Speaking and Listening

Sounds provide all sorts of useful information. Some are important warnings of danger, from a screeching fire alarm to the whine of a mosquito zooming in to bite you. (Have you ever smacked a mosquito automatically, before it even touched down on your skin? The sound of its humming wings can help you to locate it without looking.) Some sounds are promises of something good about to happen—the music of the ice cream truck heading up your block, for example. We get pleasure out of listening to music, although we don't all agree on which kinds of music are the best.

For people, some of the most important sounds are those of speech. Like other sounds, they are picked up by the sensors in the cochlea and sent up to the auditory cortex. That is not the only part of the brain involved in processing the sound messages that make up spoken words. Specialized speech areas on the cortex are located next to the ends of the auditory centers. These speech centers help in interpreting speech sounds. Learning to hear and understand spoken words allows the formation of **language**, a complex system of communication using sounds, written symbols, or gestures.

Speech Centers

In many brain functions, the two hemispheres of the brain do not play equal roles. One side becomes more developed than the other for particular activities, such as speech or drawing pictures. In general, the left hemisphere is the verbal half, which reads, writes, speaks fluently, and does difficult arithmetic. The right brain can

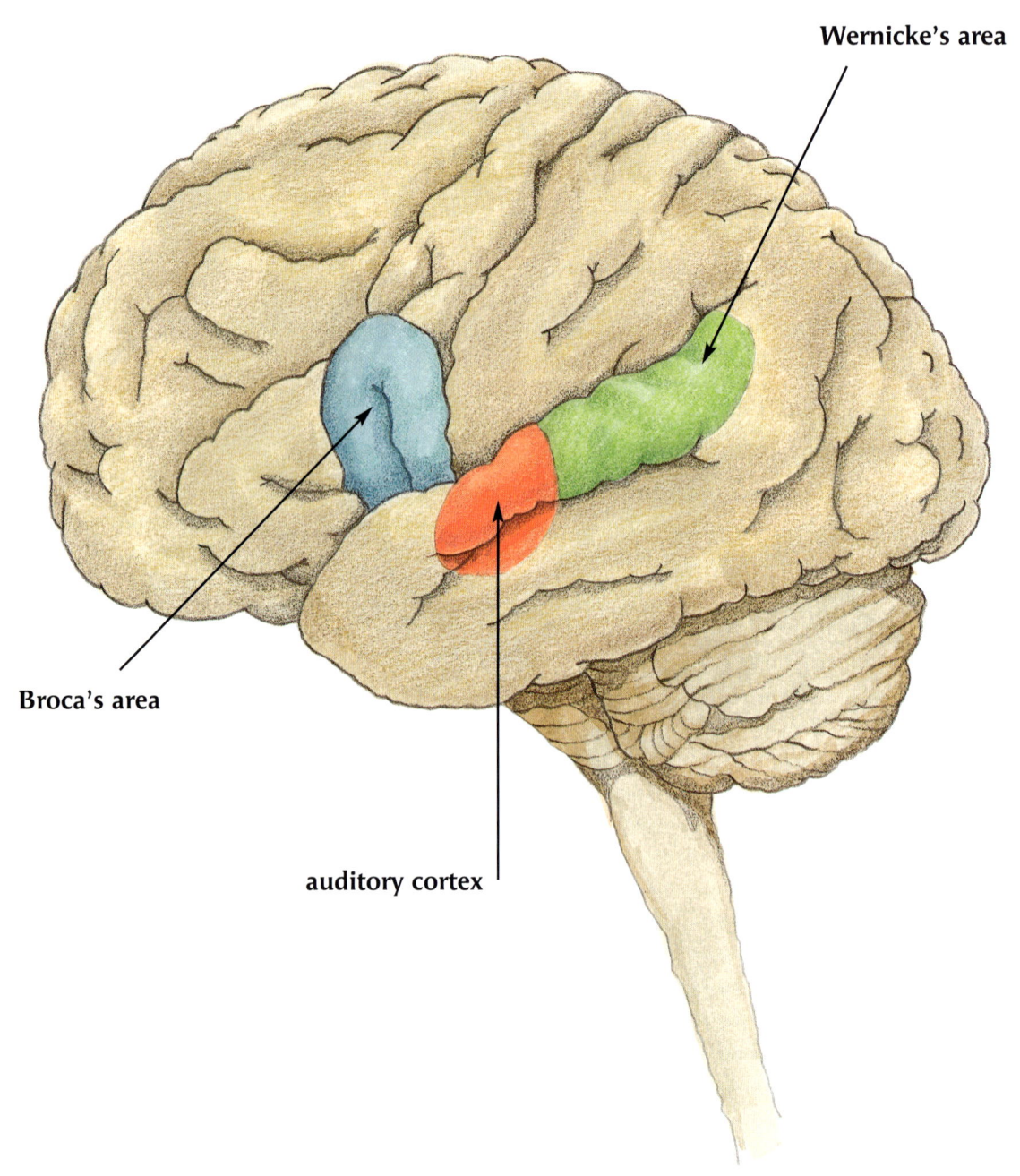

Wernicke's area and Broca's area of the brain, which are usually found only in the left hemisphere, transform sounds into meaningful speech.

read common words, do simple arithmetic, and understand simple verbal instructions. The right brain also has a keener sense of shape, form, and texture, as well as a flair for musical rhythm and melody, intuition, creativity, and a sense of humor.

The special areas in the brain that are involved in making sounds into meaningful speech are **Wernicke's area** in the temporal lobe and **Broca's area** in the frontal lobe. These vital speech centers are usually found only in the left hemisphere. Together, they help to interpret and communicate spoken words. For instance, Wernicke's area is involved in understanding the meanings of words and also strings words together to form a sentence for speaking. Broca's area directs the muscle movement so that we can speak the words once they are interpreted by Wernicke's area. The two areas work together. It has been found that patients with damage to Broca's area have lost their ability to speak. Patients with damage to Wernicke's area cannot understand what is being said.

The speech centers work with other parts of the brain so that we may connect emotions or humor to the words that we hear and speak. For instance, while watching a TV program, your main speech centers in the left hemisphere interpret the meanings of the words while the right brain deals with humor and emotional content. Listening to a song, the speech centers are concerned with the lyrics, and the right brain with the melody.

The Sounds of Speech

Like all other sounds, the sounds of speech are created by vibrations. These sound vibrations are made by **vocal cords** inside the

---

Hearing Before Birth

A baby's eyes and ears are fully developed more than five months before it is born. It cannot see anything because there is no light inside its mother's womb, but it can hear sounds transmitted through her body. An unborn baby gets so used to the sound of its mother's heartbeat that it will find a recording of a heartbeat comforting for months after it is born. It also learns to recognize the sound of its mother's voice and the voices of people who are often with her. Researchers have found that babies even learn to recognize the words and rhythm of poems or stories the mother reads out loud during her pregnancy.

With an endoscope, a doctor examines his patient's larynx, which is displayed on the television screen.

throat. The vocal cords are two folds of tissue that stretch across the **larynx** (voice box). Muscles in the larynx can tighten or loosen the vocal cords. When we speak, the muscles pull the vocal cords closer together, narrowing the opening. As we breathe and air flows out through the larynx, the tightened vocal cords vibrate, producing sounds. We can create a lot of variations in our voice: The tighter the vocal cords are stretched, the higher the sounds; the more relaxed the vocal cords, the lower the sounds. Speech sounds also vary depending on the positions of the lips and tongue.

The pitch of the voice depends on the size of the larynx. A man's vocal cords are long and thick and can produce speech sounds with a low pitch, around 120 hertz. A woman's vocal cords are thinner and shorter than a man's; her speaking voice has a higher pitch, around 220 hertz. A child's voice has an even higher pitch than a woman's. Boys and girls have roughly the same size larynx. At puberty, the larynx grows larger (and the voice gets lower) in both sexes. However, the boy's voice box grows much larger than the girl's, and the vocal cords inside get thicker and longer, making his voice lower and deeper.

Speech is made up of individual sounds that are put together to form meaningful words. People who speak the same language are able to communicate because they have learned to attach the same meanings to the various sound combinations. The words of speech are made up of units of sound, called **phonemes**—the sound of various vowel and consonant combinations. When you listen to someone speaking, the sounds are relayed from the auditory cortex in your brain to the specialized speech centers nearby. They detect the individual phonemes and recognize the words they form when they are put together in various combinations. Using this knowledge of phonemes, you can recognize words that are heard and distinguish among them, even if they are unfamiliar.

The old saying, "It's not what you say, it's how you say it," is really true. For instance, the pitch of your voice can give clues to the meaning of speech. Varying the pitch of a person's voice may also make the speaker's words sound interesting and entertaining. A **monotone** speaker, a person whose speech is mostly on a single pitch, is likely to sound boring and uninteresting.

The rising and falling of the pitch of speech sounds is called **intonation**. In the English language, intonations are used to put emphasis on certain words that can change the meaning of the sentence. For example, a question, an exclamation, or a statement could be conveyed by the same words, pronounced with different intonations. Even a simple word, such as "no," can have several different meanings depending on the way it is spoken.

How fast a person talks can also provide information. People tend to talk more quickly when they are excited and more slowly when they are being very serious or sad.

Loudness is another important cue to speech. Variations in loudness put emphasis on certain words and syllables. In the word

DID YOU KNOW?

We usually speak while exhaling. Although it is possible to talk while inhaling, it is difficult, and the voice sounds strange and unnatural.

> **DID YOU KNOW?**
>
> The average speaking rate is 150 words per minute. The world record for fast talking is 637 words in 60 seconds.

"loudness," for example, the first syllable is considerably louder than the second. We also adjust our voices automatically when we are competing with other noises, such as traffic on a busy street or other conversations going on in the same room. Loudness can also express anger or excitement in a person's voice.

Everybody is born with the ability to learn language. In infants, nerve cells in the brain are not well connected yet. Early in life, children can hear and distinguish the sounds of any language in the world. But as they grow and hear the sounds of their native language, the cells in their brains make connections based on the frequency of the sounds spoken around them. Each time the same connection is made, those particular circuits are strengthened. Eventually, as connections in the hearing and speech centers become devoted more and more to the sounds of the language the child hears constantly, the ability to distinguish *all* speech sounds is lost. A native Japanese speaker, for example, becomes unable to distinguish between the sounds of *r* and *l* as they are pronounced in English, because only an *r* sound occurs in spoken Japanese. So the typical Japanese speaker cannot tell the difference between the words "right" and "light." And because speaking words requires the ability to hear distinctions between their phonemes, Japanese speakers would tend to pronounce both words as "right," or to say the word "really" as though it were spelled "reery."

With each passing year in a child's life, learning the sounds of another language becomes more difficult. In fact, scientists have found that few people can learn to speak a new language without an accent after the age of ten. Recent studies have shown, however, that with very intensive training, people can learn to distinguish particular pairs of "problem sounds" in foreign languages, such as the English *r* and *l* for a native Japanese speaker. But each pair of words must be drilled and learned individually.

Speech Recognition Technology

Human speech is more than just the ability to make sounds that are grouped into recognizable words. Speech also involves *listening*—hearing, recognizing, and understanding the sounds of spoken language. Computer scientists have developed machines that recognize speech, too. These machines, known as speech recognition systems, are becoming widely available to businesses and individuals. Computerized speech recognition systems are programmed to recognize certain words or phrases in their databanks. Early systems had to be trained to the voice of each individual user, who had to speak slowly, only one word at a time. Today's speech recognition systems are more advanced: They recognize phonemes, making it possible to distinguish between words much more accurately and quickly.

Speech recognition systems are a growing part of our everyday lives. When you call a business on the phone, you may be greeted by a computerized "menu" offering you a series of choices to which you can answer "yes" or "no," or respond by saying numbers like "one" or "two," to get to the person or service you want to reach. Telephone companies use speech recognition systems for calling services. For instance, the computer can recognize such phrases as "collect," "person-to-person," or "operator," spoken by people of varied ages and regional accents. The latest models of VCRs and TVs have speech recognition systems to allow voice input of commands to activate the VCR to tape television programs or operate various TV controls.

Speech recognition systems are very effective for simple jobs that require a limited vocabulary. But more complicated systems, such as those designed for dictation, may involve

Voice Prints

You can tell a lot about a person by the way he or she talks. Everybody has a characteristic pattern of speech, similar to a unique fingerprint. A device called a **spectrograph** is designed to analyze a person's voice and break down the varying sounds, which are displayed on a graph.

Spectrograms (the recordings made from spectrographs) may be used in criminal investigations to get a positive identification on a suspect or to check for lying. These "voice prints" show the pitch and loudness of each syllable, and their variations can even reveal the person's state of mind and emotions. The pitch tends to be higher, for example, when a person is excited or stressed—as when telling a lie. But spectrograms do not make very good lie detectors. They may give inaccurate readings for people who are naturally nervous and also for people who are good liars and show no change in emotional readings.

Voice prints are also used in security systems. A person is asked to speak an identifying phrase, and a computer matches up the person's voice readings to those stored in the database. A positive ID allows access to restricted areas.

A man uses a specially designed computer workstation that is controlled by his voice. This kind of speech recognition system has been used to allow paralyzed people to control devices such as lights, televisions, radios, door openers, telephones, and more.

some problems. Word pronunciation varies from one region to another; there are also individual differences between one person and another. You can sometimes tell where someone comes from by the way they pronounce key words. For instance, Canadians pronounce the word "about" as "aboat," and people from Scotland would say "aboot." A native New Yorker tends to put an *r* at the end of certain words, such as "idear" for idea, and "sawr" for saw; Southerners tend to drop the final *r*, saying "suh" for "sir." Computers that "listen" to these phonemes would spell the words as they sound, which is not always the correct spelling. Therefore, speech recognition systems used for dictation still require the user to spend some time working with the program at first, saying various words and phrases and correcting errors as the computer learns how the person pronounces particular phonemes.

FIVE
The Sound of Music

Do you know the "Happy Birthday" song? Of course you do. You've probably heard it since you were a baby. Music is one of the most powerful kinds of sounds. It sticks with us. We can hear a piece of music, and a stream of memories will rush in. We may remember some good times we had with friends or a painful breakup with a boyfriend or girlfriend.

Music is similar to speech in that it allows us to express our ideas, thoughts, and feelings. Music is actually a combination of sounds put together in a pattern with three important elements: melody, rhythm, and harmony. A **melody** is a series of sounds with different pitches or tones. **Rhythm** is the pacing—the rate at which the sounds are played or sung and the length of time and relative loudness of each tone. **Harmony** is a combination of different tones that are played together so that they make a pleasing sound (a chord).

Listening to music can produce emotional reactions, from mild feelings of pleasure or relaxation to intense joy, sorrow, or excitement. Our reactions to particular kinds of music, like our understanding of language, are partly determined by the culture in which we grow up. But the ability to produce music and respond to it is part of the basic "equipment" we inherit, the specialized neurons of the brain.

Music in the Brain

There is no single "music center" in the brain. Instead, many parts of the brain are involved in processing music. The left hemisphere contains areas that specialize in recognizing language, and the right hemisphere has areas that focus on music perception. But studies have shown that language and music have some shared pathways in the brain.

It makes sense that language and music are somehow connected. The auditory centers on both sides of the head have special cells that can recognize and process pitch, determining the

Many parts of the brain are involved in processing music. The ability to play music and how we respond to it is partly genetic and partly determined by the environment in which we grow up.

Many different emotions are roused when people listen to music. Musicians can use this knowledge to evoke desired responses.

patterns in the frequencies of sound vibrations. When we listen to music, we use many of the same pitch detectors that we use in listening to a person speaking.

Do you ever find that a particular song keeps playing in your mind? It seems almost as though you are hearing it, but your ears are not picking up sound vibrations. It is all in your brain. We can

What Is Perfect Pitch?

If you hear a musical tone, can you tell what note it is? In music, the sounds produced by the voice or by an instrument are each assigned a place in a sequence, or **scale**. In an orchestra, all the instruments must be tuned the same; otherwise, they could not play in harmony.

Musicians and singers may use a tool called a pitch pipe (a sort of harmonica) to tune their instruments or adjust their voices. But some people have perfect pitch, the ability to tell what note corresponds to a sound they hear, even without first listening to a reference note such as the A of a pitch pipe. Most people have relative pitch: When they hear musical notes, they can mentally fit them into a scale, although they may not know which scale it is in terms of sound frequencies.

Researchers are not sure whether perfect pitch is an inborn talent or something that is developed with training, but they have found some physical differences in the brain's hearing centers. In one study, German scientists compared the brains of thirty musicians (eleven of whom had perfect pitch) to those of thirty nonmusicians, using special brain imaging scanners. They found that part of the auditory cortex in musicians with perfect pitch was more developed in the left hemisphere than in the right. There was no noticeable size difference in nonmusicians and in musicians without perfect pitch. In addition, the corpus callosum, the thick cable of nerve fibers that connects the two hemispheres, was 10 to 15 percent thicker in musicians with perfect pitch than in nonmusicians or late-blooming musicians.

imagine music because the brain has stored the many songs, melodies, and sounds of instruments from your past experiences into your memory. When we "imagine" a song, the cells and circuits in our brain become activated just as if we were actually hearing

Did You Know?

Many physicists and mathematicians are also talented musicians.

music coming from the outside world. Oddly enough, parts of our visual cortex (the seeing center) also become activated, which implies that our brains link up the sounds of melodies with visual images.

Music is processed primarily in the right hemisphere. Scientists have found that the music networks run into the emotional circuits in the right brain. People may feel a variety of emotions when they listen to music. The sounds in a song may give you goosebumps, make you feel like you have a lump in your throat, cause deep sadness, or make you feel like jumping for joy.

Music can be good medicine. Hospitals and rehabilitation centers use it in patients' treatment programs. Music with soothing melodies can help people relax; tunes with a rhythmic beat may stimulate the brain systems that control muscle movements and the secretions of glands, and make exercise programs more effective. Music can benefit people with a wide variety of illnesses and injuries, including strokes. Older people who are taught to play music are less likely to suffer from depression, anxiety, or feelings of loneliness.

The Intelligence Link

Can music make you smarter? Some researchers have found that early musical training may help strengthen nerve connections in the brain and even make new ones.

In one study, a researcher worked with two groups of three-year-olds in Los Angeles, California. One group of children had weekly piano lessons and daily sessions of group singing. Another group did not receive any extra musical training. After a year of this program, the musically trained children scored 80 percent higher on tests of spatial ability (the ability to perceive the shapes of objects and their relative positions in space) and mathematical problem solving.

Scientists say that children should start their musical training before the age of twelve to improve their learning ability. But some controversial experiments with college students who listened to Mozart sonatas showed improvements in spatial and math skills, even if they didn't like Mozart. The authors of the study say that

Some scientists believe that musical training at a young age can improve a child's learning ability, mathematical skills, and other aptitudes.

the complicated structure of Mozart's music helps to develop the brain connections involved in thought and reasoning processes. Other researchers could not repeat these findings and criticized the way the study was conducted.

Although many scientists believe the "Mozart effect" does not really exist, marketers quickly turned it into a popular fad. Parents can now buy "Make Your Baby Smarter" CDs with Mozart and other classical music, and the state of Georgia funded a program that gives a classical music tape or CD to every baby born in the state.

SIX
Seeing With Sound

> **Did You Know?**
>
> Bats can hear and produce ultrasounds up to 100,000 hertz. (Remember, humans can hear only up to about 20,000 hertz.)

If you walked into your well-lighted bedroom, you could clearly see everything: your desk covered with books and papers; a skateboard and clothes in the middle of the floor; poster-covered walls; an unmade bed. Your eyes work so well that you could easily walk from the door to the bed, detouring carefully around the mess in the middle of the floor. But what if the bedroom were dark? Would you be able to avoid the things on the floor? Probably not.

Our eyes need light rays to focus so we can get a clear picture of our surroundings. This allows us to see where we are going and avoid obstacles. But this is not the only way to "see." Bats, for instance, can find their way in the dark without using their eyes—they use their ears. Through a process called **echolocation**, bats can "see" by interpreting the way sound waves bounce off objects. Whales and dolphins use echolocation to see things in the ocean.

Scientists have learned a great deal about seeing with sound by studying animals such as bats and dolphins. They used this knowledge to create **sonar**, a method to detect and locate underwater objects using sound waves.

Sonar Systems in Nature

Even on the darkest nights, bats can snatch up tiny insects and fly about in their crowded, pitch-black caves without bumping into anything. In research studies, scientists found that a bat can easily fly through a darkened room in which very thin, dangling wires hang from the ceiling only a wingspan apart, without even brushing against the wires. In total darkness, a bat can not only catch mealworms thrown up into the air, but also can tell whether its prey is a mealworm or only a small stick of the same size.

If a bat is blindfolded, it can still find its way perfectly well. But if its ears are plugged or its nose or mouth is taped up, it blunders around helplessly, bumping into things. That is because it must both produce and hear sounds to use its echolocation system effectively. Through its nose or mouth, the bat sends out a series of very high-pitched ultrasounds. If there is anything in its path, the sound waves bounce off and return as echoes. The bat's large ears funnel in the returning sound echoes and send messages to its brain. The part of the bat's brain that deals with analyzing sounds is larger and better developed than any other part of its brain. The auditory centers of the bat's cerebrum put together the patterns of the echoes and form mental "pictures" of the surroundings. In a split second, the bat can figure out what kind of object the echoes bounced off, how far away it is, and how it is moving. The bat's brain is so efficient that it can locate prey as tiny as a mosquito and plot a flight path to intercept it.

Echolocation is used extensively in the water by other sonar experts— dolphins and whales. They navigate through dark, murky waters, avoiding obstacles and danger and locating prey with a sonar system very much like that of bats. Bats, however, give off pulses of ultrasound during echolocation, while dolphins give off clicking sounds that contain both audible and ultrasonic frequencies.

> ## Sonar's Sister System: Radar
> **Radar** works in much the same way as sonar. *Radar*, named for *ra*dio *d*etection *a*nd *r*anging, uses radio waves to detect and locate objects that are too distant for the human eye to see. The radar system sends out radio waves, which are reflected when they strike an object and return as echoes, just like the sound waves in the sonar system. Radar is very effective at night and in poor weather conditions such as heavy fog, rain, or snow.
>
> Air traffic controllers depend on radar to track and guide airplanes for landing at busy airports or during bad weather. It is widely used in ship navigation, especially in avoiding obstacles when the visibility is poor during bad weather conditions. Radar also has military uses. It can detect and track an approaching enemy airplane at great distances. Police officers use radar to detect speeding cars. A radar gun records the frequency difference of radio waves when they bounce off the moving vehicle.

Sonar Technology

The sonar systems of bats and dolphins are so effective that scientists have created artificial sonar systems. People can now "see" in areas where it was once impossible, such as the ocean. The word *sonar*, which comes from the phrase *so*und *n*avigation *a*nd *r*anging, was designed to detect and locate underwater objects by sound location.

There are two main kinds of systems: active sonar and passive sonar. Active sonar sends out a sharp pulse of sound very much like a "ping." This pulse is reflected back when it hits an object. The

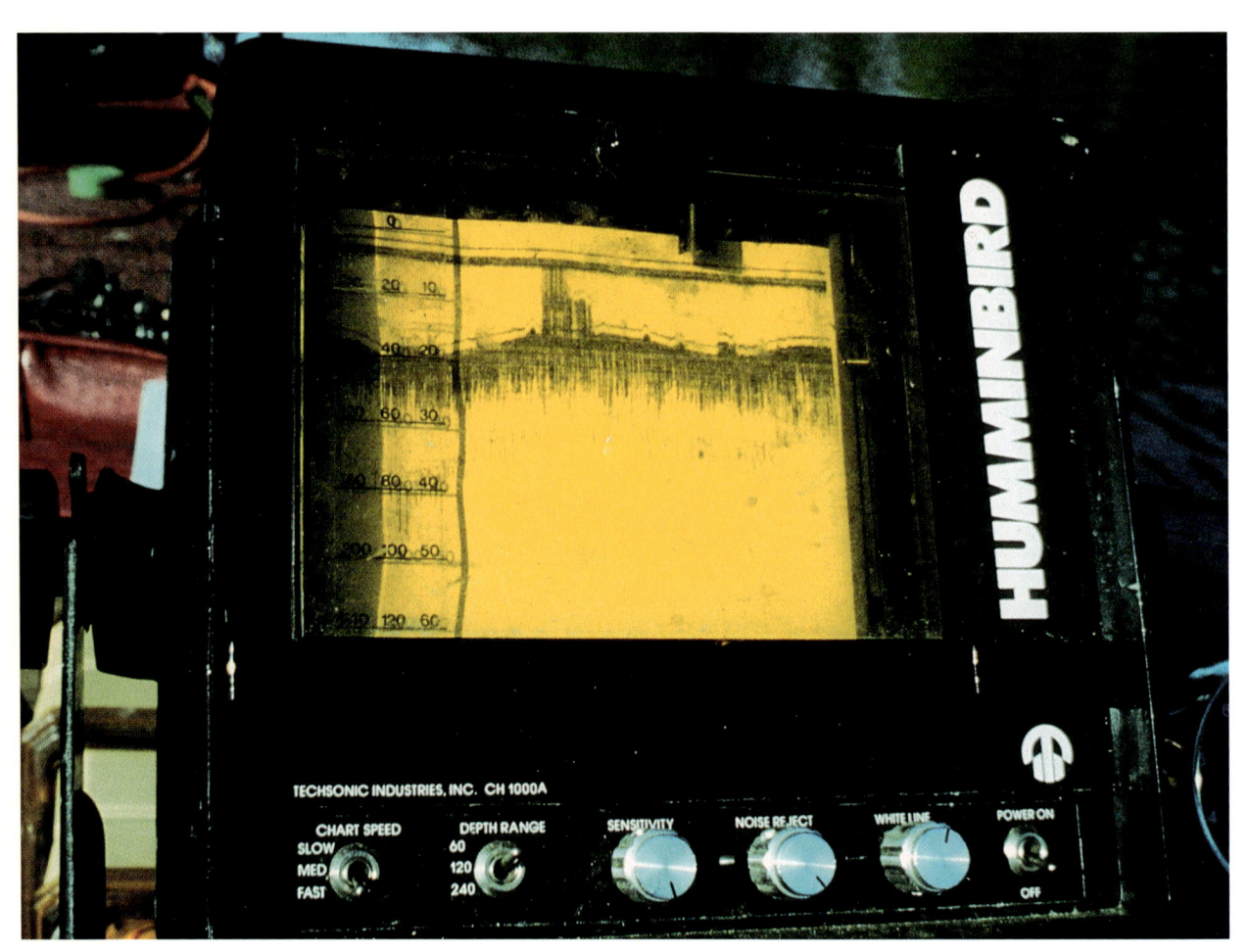

Sonar systems have many different uses: to help ships navigate, map the ocean bottom, locate wrecks, identify and locate enemy ships and submarines, detect mines, and locate fish for commercial fishing. The system shown here records the vessel's depth.

sonar system determines how far the object is by the amount of time it takes for the sound to come back to the ship. For instance, sound travels about 5,000 feet (1,500 meters) per second through water. If an echo returns after two seconds, the object is 5,000 feet away. (The sound waves took one second to get to the object and one second to get back.)

Passive sonar systems use receiving sensors that can pick up the sounds given off by other ships or submarines. The sound waves are analyzed by special equipment, which can identify the ship that produced the sound and determine its direction, speed, and distance. Passive sonar does not send out its own sounds to navigate or locate an object. Such signals might bring in more information, but they could be picked up by the sonar units of enemy ships. Using passive sonar, a ship can "see" while remaining hidden.

Human Sonar

Some humans also use echo-location. Blind people may make a variety of sounds, such as hisses, tongue clicks, finger snaps, and tapping a cane, to help them find their way around. They analyze the reflected sound waves to avoid obstacles in much the same way as bats and dolphins. They can learn to tell the size and shape of objects. In one experiment, blind people were found to be able to sense the presence of a target less than 2 inches (5 cm) wide at about 2 feet (0.6 m) away, and a 10-inch (25-cm) target at about 9 feet (2.7 m) away, using their own sonar.

SEVEN
Too Much Sound?

> **Did You Know?**
>
> In the gradual loss of hearing that often occurs with aging, the ability to hear higher-pitched sounds typically goes first. So an older person may have trouble understanding female news commentators on radio or TV while male voices seem clear.

Do you like to pump up the volume or go to loud concerts? These days, people are surrounded by loud sounds: amplified bands at concerts; blaring fire engine sirens; high-pitched train whistles; thundering trucks on the highway; high-powered lawnmowers; soaring jet airplanes. Sounds like these are often too loud for our ears to handle.

Our ears are effective tools for collecting sounds. They are so sensitive that we can hear anything from a soft whisper to a loud jet engine. But too much sound, especially loud sounds, can cause hearing problems.

What Is Noise?

Have you ever cranked up your stereo only to hear your mom or dad yell, "Turn that *noise* down!" Your parents consider your loud music to be noise, but you enjoy it. **Noise** is defined as unwanted sound. But noise is really subjective—what is noise to one person may be a pleasant sound to another, especially when it comes to music. Noises may range from quiet sounds to loud sounds. Loud noises can cause damage to a person's hearing.

What happens when loud sounds enter our ears? Normally, we hear sounds when the vibrations cause the sound sensors, the hair cells in the organ of Corti, to bend back and forth. A loud noise excites more hair cells than a softer noise. The hair cells also bend much farther with louder noises. The bending of the hair cells releases a chemical that sends a message along the auditory nerve to the brain. If the noise is too loud, the hair cells become flattened and are not activated. If the exposure to a loud noise is brief—for example, if a person hears a gunshot close by—the hair cells usually recover fairly quickly, and the hearing returns to normal. Very long or repeated exposure to loud noises, however, can make the hair cells less flexible or even kill them. Once the hair cells are gone, they don't come back. This can cause permanent hearing loss.

Since we do live in a world filled with noise, we need to protect our ears. Ear protection may range from tiny earplugs to cover the ear canal to earmuffs, which cover the ear entirely. Most ear protectors can reduce the noise level by 20 to 30 dB. In the United States, laws require workers who are exposed to sound levels greater than 90 dB to wear some form of ear protection.

Unfortunately, not all causes of hearing loss are this preventable. Some people are born hearing-impaired or deaf. Others may lose their hearing due to serious ear infections, illnesses, or trauma.

> ## How Loud Is Too Loud?
> The loudness of sound is measured in decibels (dB). How loud are the sounds you hear every day?
>
> - Watch ticking — 20 dB
> - Whispering — 30 dB
> - Leaves rustling, refrigerator — 40 dB
> - Normal conversation, dishwasher, microwave oven — 60 dB
> - Car, alarm clock, city traffic — 70 dB
> - Vacuum cleaner, garbage disposal, noisy restaurant — 80 dB
> - Lawn mower, passing motorcycle — 90 dB
> - Chain saw, blow-dryer, snowmobile — 100 dB
> - Car horn, snowblower — 110 dB
> - Jackhammer, rock concert — 120 dB
> - Jet engine at 100 feet away — 130 dB
> - Shotgun blast — 140 dB
>
> Studies in which the hearing of factory workers was measured before and after several months of work under high-noise conditions have shown that prolonged exposure to noise above 85 to 90 dB can damage hearing.

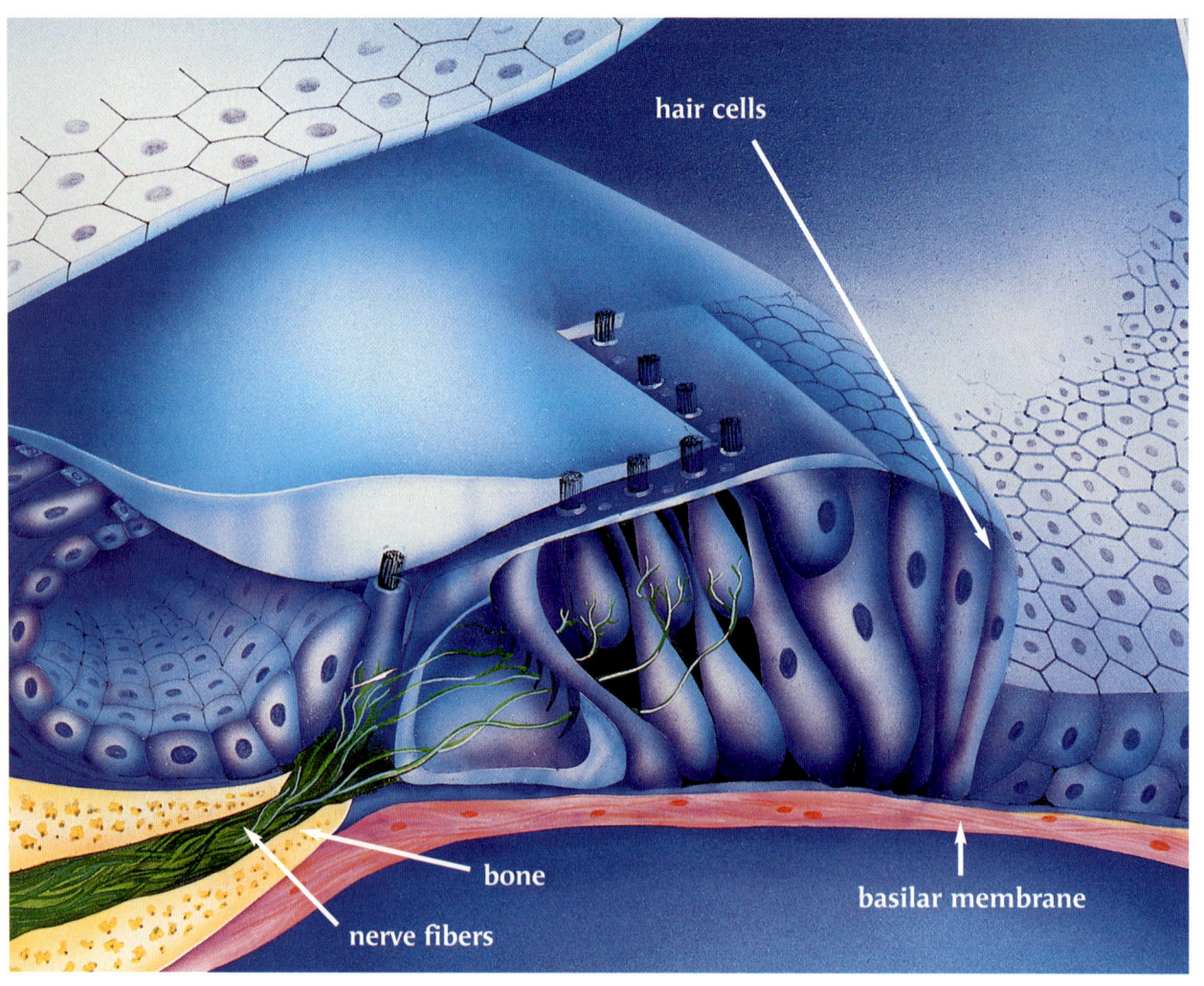

This illustration of the organ of Corti shows the nerve fibers (green) that run through the bone (yellow) to the hair cells supported by the basilar membrane (red). Vibrations are transmitted to the hair cells that generate nervous impulses, which then pass to the brain.

Electronic Ears

Helen Keller, who lost both her sight and her hearing after a serious childhood illness, was once asked which of her senses she would most like to have restored if that could be done. She replied immediately, "Hearing, because it truly connects you to the world."

People who develop hearing problems may feel insecure and disconnected from the world. They often have trouble communicating with their family and friends—they ask others to repeat themselves and miss key words that give meaning to conversations. To a person who is hearing-impaired, speech sounds like a lot of mumbling.

Researchers have been working hard developing devices that can help the hearing impaired and even people who are completely deaf. Hearing aids are the most commonly used listening devices. A hearing aid will not restore a person's hearing ability, but it will make the sounds louder and clearer. Its design involves a microphone, which picks up the sound and turns it into an electric signal; an amplifier, which makes the signal louder and clearer; a receiver, which turns the signal back into sound; and a device that delivers the sound into the ear.

Although hearing aids do improve hearing, they have some disadvantages. Hearing aids cannot restore a person's ability to hear all frequencies, especially high-frequency sounds. So the person often cannot hear certain spoken words clearly. Another common complaint is that the hearing aid picks up *all* sounds, including those in the background. So trying to have a conversation in a crowded restaurant can be very frustrating.

Recently, more sophisticated devices have been designed to improve hearing and greatly reduce the problem of background noise. These devices, called digital hearing aids, are adapted to the individual. The digital hearing aid uses a

Do You Hear What I Hear?

When you have your hearing tested, you put on a headphone and are asked whether you hear each of a series of tones of different pitches. But how can doctors find out whether a newborn baby can hear properly? The infant would not understand such questions, much less be able to answer them. And yet, it is very important to detect and treat hearing problems as early as possible, so that language and social skills can develop normally. Infants just a few weeks old can be fitted with hearing aids, and a cochlear implant can be used after the age of 18 months.

Doctors use two kinds of screening tests to detect the one in 1,000 babies born with serious hearing problems. In auditory brainstem response tests, electrodes pasted behind the baby's ears measure electrical activity in the brain in response to sounds. In otoacoustic emissions tests, small probes are placed in the baby's ear canals. These probes detect tiny audio signals produced by the hair cells in the cochlea in response to sounds.

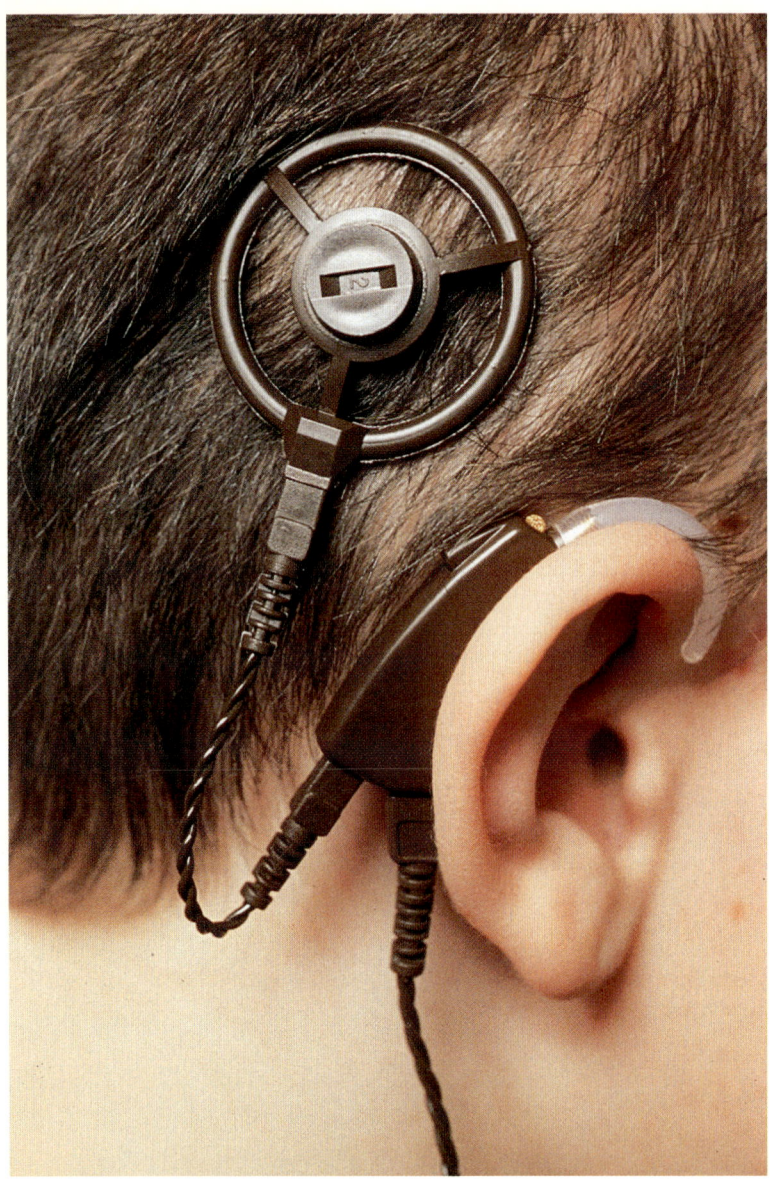

The cochlear implant shown here includes a transmitter fitted to the girl's head and a microphone positioned behind her ear.

powerful computer chip specially programmed to the hearing of the person who is wearing the device. It amplifies the sounds that the hearing-impaired person is lacking and filters out the background noise.

Since a hearing aid's job is to make sounds louder, it cannot help people who are completely deaf. The **cochlear implant** is a surgically implanted device that can help people who have severe hearing loss. This device is designed for people who have severely damaged hair cells but some functioning auditory nerve cells that can send sound signals to the brain. Here's how it works: Sounds are picked up by an external microphone and are then sent along a wire to a speech processor, where they are turned into coded electrical signals. The coded signals are sent from the speech processor through tiny cables to a transmitting coil, which sends the signals through the skin to the receiver/stimulator, which is implanted behind the ear. The receiver/stimulator sends the signals to electrodes implanted in the cochlea. These electrodes stimulate the auditory nerve to carry the electrical signals to the brain, where they are interpreted as sound.

People with cochlear implants do not hear the same sounds that a person with normal hearing hears. They must learn to interpret what they are hearing, and they may require special speech training. This procedure is more likely to benefit people who could hear and speak before becoming deaf than those who had never heard or learned to speak at all. Unfortunately, these implants cannot help people who are deaf because of damage to the auditory nerves or the hearing centers in the brain. Yet, artificial sensors, along with computer technology, are constantly enhancing our ability to use our natural senses.

Glossary

air bladder—gas-filled sac in fish, which picks up sound vibrations

auditory cortex—the hearing center; the part of the brain that controls hearing

auditory nerve—a thick cord of nerve cells that send nerve signals from the ears to the brain, where they are translated into meaningful sounds

basilar membrane—a membrane on the floor of the cochlea in the inner ear

binaural hearing—listening with two ears

Broca's area—speech center in the brain's frontal lobe that directs muscle movement so we can speak words once they are interpreted by Wernicke's area

cerebral cortex—the thin, outermost layer of the brain where most of the activity in the brain takes place

cerebrum—the largest part of the brain, with which we think, remember, process sensory information, make decisions, and control the movements of the body

cochlea—fluid-filled spiral-shaped tube in the inner ear that contains the organ for hearing; looks like a snail shell

cochlear implant—an electronic device that picks up sounds and converts them to electrical signals, which are transmitted to electrodes surgically implanted in the cochlea and which stimulate the auditory nerve

compression waves—sound waves, which travel by condensing the medium through which they move

corpus collosum—a thick cable of nerve fibers deep inside the brain that link the two brain hemispheres and permit an exchange of information between them

decibel (dB)—a unit to measure the loudness of sound

ear canal—a curved tube leading into the ear

eardrums—the vibrating membranes that stretch across the openings into our ears

echolocation—method used by bats, dolphins, and other animals to detect objects by sending out high-pitched sounds that bounce off the object and come back to the animal's ears

frequency—the number of waves that pass a given point in a certain time

hair sensilla—tiny, hairlike sound-detecting structures on certain insects

harmony—a combination of different tones played together that make a pleasing sound (a chord)

hemispheres—two halves of the brain, the left and the right

hertz—a unit of sound frequency

infrasound—sound energy with a frequency lower than humans can hear

intonation—the rising and falling of pitch in speech

invertebrates—animals without backbones or an internal skeleton

language—a complex system of communication using sounds, written symbols, or gestures

larynx—voice box

melody—a series of sounds with different pitches or tones

monaural hearing—listening with only one ear

monotone—speaking mostly on a single pitch

neurons—nerve cells

noise—unwanted sound

organ of Corti—a structure that rests on the basilar membrane in the inner ear; contains thousands of sound-sensitive hairs

oval window—the membrane that covers the entrance to the inner ear

phonemes—units of sound in speech

pinna (*plural* pinnae)—outer ear; it has a large earflap and narrow opening

pitch—how high or low a sound is; determined by the sound frequency

radar—uses radio waves to detect and locate objects that are too far for the human eye to see; often used in airplane and ship navigation

reticular activating system (RAS)—a network of nerve fibers in the brain that screens all the incoming messages from the senses and sends on only those that seem unusual, interesting, or important

rhythm—in music, the rate at which the sounds are played or sung and the length of time of each tone

scale—in music, sounds assigned a place in a sequence

sensors—specialized structures that gather information about the world; they detect various types of energy and transmit signals to the brain

sonar—sound location; a method to detect and locate underwater objects using sound waves

spectrograph—a device designed to analyze a person's voice and break down the varying sounds, which are displayed visually on a spectrogram

tympanic membrane—*see* eardrum

ultrasound—sound energy with a frequency higher than humans can hear

vertebrates—animals with backbones and an internal skeleton

vibration—back-and-forth movement, e.g., of a plucked guitar string

vocal cords—folds of tissue in the larynx that produce sound vibrations

wavelength—the distance between the top of one wave and the top of the next

Wernicke's area—speech center in the brain's temporal lobe that understands the meaning of words and strings together words to form a sentence for speaking

Further Reading

Barré, Michel. *Animal Senses*. Milwaukee, Wis.: Gareth Stevens Publishing, 1998.

Cobb, Vicki. *How to Really Fool Yourself: Illusions for All Your Senses*. New York: John Wiley & Sons, Inc., 1999.

Hay, Jennifer. *Hearing Loss: Questions You Have . . . Answers You Need*. Allentown, Pa.: People's Medical Society, 1994.

Hellman, Hal. *Beyond Your Senses: The New World of Sensors*. New York: Lodestar Books, 1997.

Hickman, Pamela. *Animal Senses: How Animals See, Hear, Taste, Smell, and Feel*. Buffalo, N.Y.: Kids Can Press Ltd., 1998.

Llamas, Andreu. *The Five Senses of the Animal World: Hearing*. New York: Chelsea House Publishers, 1995.

Parker, Steve. *Look at Your Body: Senses*. Brookfield, Conn.: Copper Beech Books, 1997.

Santa Fe Writers Group. *Bizarre & Beautiful Ears*. Santa Fe, N. Mex.: John Muir Publications, 1993.

Silverstein, Alvin and Virginia. *Wonders of Speech*. New York: William Morrow, 1988.

Tytla, Milan. *See Hear: Playing with Light and Sound*. Toronto, Ont.: Annick Press Ltd., 1994.

Internet Resources

www.betterhearing.org/
Better Hearing Institute's Hearing Help-On-Line

www.betterhearing.org/faq.htm
FAQ about People with Hearing Loss, Better Hearing Institute

www.hhmi.org/senses
"Seeing, Hearing, and Smelling the World: New Findings Help Scientists Make Sense of Our Senses," The Howard Hughes Medical Institute

www.listen-up.org/resources.htm
The Listen-Up Web

www.omi.tulane.edu/departments/pathology/fermin/Hearing.html
The Incredible Sense of Hearing

www.science.wayne.edu/~)wpoff/cor/sen/hearing.html
HyperText Psychology—Senses/Hearing

www.usnews.com/usnews/issue/990426/nycu/26hear.htm
"What'd You Say? A high-volume world takes a toll on ever younger ears," Linda Kulman, US News Online, April 1999

Index

Page numbers in *italics* refer to illustrations.

Acoustic microscopes, 11
Active sonar, 48–49
Air bladder, 16
Air molecules, 12–15
Amphibians, 16–17, *17*
Animals
    hearing of, 10, *11*, 15–19, 28
Anvil, 20, *21*
Artificial sensors, 10–11
Astronauts, 15
Auditory brainstem response tests, 53
Auditory cortex, 26, 31, *32*, 35, 43
Auditory nerve, 19, *21*, 22, 24, 54–55

Basilar membrane, 21, *22*, 26, *52*
Bats, 10, *11*, 15, 16, 19, 28, 46–47
Binaural hearing, 28
Birds, *18*, 19
Blind people, 49

Brain, 12, 22, 24–30, *25*, *26*
    auditory cortex, 26, 31, *32*, 35, 43
    cerebral cortex, *25*, 25, 26, 30
    cerebrum, *25*, 25
    hemispheres of, 25–26, *27*, 31, *32*, 33, 41, 43, 44
    music and, 41–44
    reticular activating system (RAS), *29*, 30
    speech centers, 31, *32*, 33
Brain stem, *25*
Broca's area, *32*, 33

Cerebral cortex, *25*, 25, 26, 30
Cerebrum, *25*, 25
Cochlea, 19–21, *21*, 26, 31, 53
Cochlear implant, 53–55, *54*
Compression waves, 13, 14
Computerized speech recognition systems, 36–37, *38*, 39
Consonants, 35
Corpus callosum, 25, *26*, 43
Crickets, 16
Crocodiles, 19

Decibels (dB), 51
Digital hearing aids, 53–54
Dogs, 15, 19, 28
Dolphins, 10, 15, 46, 47

Ear canal, 20, *21*
Eardrum, 12, 16, 19, 20, *21*
Ear protection, 51
Echolocation, 46–47, 49
Elephants, 15
Endoscope, 34, *34*
External ear, 19–20

Fish, 16
Foxes, 19
Frequency, *14*, 14–15
Frogs, 16–17, *17*
Frontal lobe, *25*, 33

Gender, hearing and, 28

Hair cells, 21–22, 50–51, *52*
Hair sensilla, 16
Hammer, 20, *21*
Harmony, 40
Hearing
    of amphibians, 16–17, *17*
    of bats, 10, *11*, 15, 16, 19, 28, 46–47
    binaural, 28
    before birth, 33
    brain and (*see* Brain)
    echolocation, 46–47, 49
    gender and, 28
    loss, 50–55
    monaural, 28
    of reptiles, 17–19
    of whales and dolphins, 10, 15, 46, 47
Hearing aids, 53–54

Hemispheres of brain, 25–26, *27*, 31, *32*, 33, 41, 43, 44
Hertz, 14–15, 34–35, 46
Hippopotamus, 19
Horses, 19, 28

Infrasound, 15
Inner ear, 20–21
Insects, 16
Intonation, 35
Invertebrates, 16

Keller, Helen, 52

Language, 31, 35, 36
Larynx (voice box), *34*, 34–35
Left hemisphere of brain, 25–26, *27*, 31, *32*, 33, 41, 43
Lie detectors, 37
Light energy, 13
Listening, 36

Melody, 40
Membranes, 16
Microscopes, 11
Monaural hearing, 28
Monotone, 35
Mosquitoes, 16
Moths, 16
Mozart effect, 44–45
Music, *8*, 40–45, *41*, *42*, *45*
Musical training, 44–45, *45*

Neurons, 25
Noise, defined, 50

Occipital lobe, *25*
Organ of Corti, 21–22, *22*, 50, *52*
Otoacoustic emissions tests, 53
Oval window, 20, *21*

63

Owls, 10

Parietal lobe, *25*
Passive sonar, 48, 49
Phonemes, 35–37, 39
Pinnae, 19
Pitch, 15, 35, 41–43
Pitch pipe, 43

Rabbits, 19, *20*
Radar, 47
Radio waves, 15, 23, 47
Reptiles, 17–19
Reticular activating system (RAS), *29*, 30
Rhythm, 40
Right hemisphere of brain, 25–26, *27*, 31, 33, 41, 43, 44

Scale (musical), 43
Sea lions, 19
Sensors, 10
Ship navigation, 47, *48*, 49
Smell, sense of, 9
Snakes, 18–19
Sonar, 10–11, 46–49, *48*
Songbirds, *18*, 19
Sound (*see also* Speech)
    defined, 12–14
    detectors, 15–19
    infrasound, 15
    loudness of, 50–51
    pitch, 15
    reproducing, 23
    ultrasound, 11, 15, 16, 22–23, 46, 47
    waves, *13*, 13–15
Space, silence in, 15

Spectrograms, 37
Spectrograph, 37
Speech
    centers in brain, 31, *32*, 33, 35
    loudness, 35–36
    phonemes and, 35–37, 39
    rate of, 36
    sounds of, 33–36
Speech recognition technology, 36–37, *38*, 39
Stereo sound, 28
Stethoscope, 22
Stirrup, 2–7

Tape recordings, 28
Taste, sense of, 9
Temporal lobe, *25*, 26, 33
Thalamus, *25*
Toads, 16–17
Touching, 9
Tympanic membrane (eardrum), 12, 16, 19, 20, *21*

Ultrasound, 11, 15, 16, 22–23, 46, 47

Vertebrates, 16
Vibration, 12
Vision, 9
Visual cortex, 44
Vocal cords, 33–35
Voice box, 12, *34*, 34–35
Voice prints, 37
Vowels, 35

Wavelengths, 14
Wernicke's area, *32*, 33
Whales, 10, 15, 46, 47